Sandy Klop

American Jane's
Quilts for
All Seasons
...and Some for No Reason

Martingale®
& C O M P A N Y

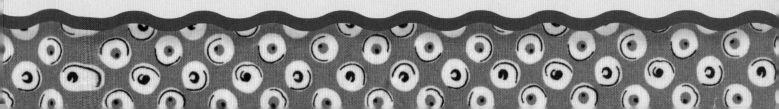

Dedication

To Stan, my husband, partner, and friend. He was a sprinter in college, but he has learned endurance with me, as we worked together to produce this book.

Acknowledgments

I'd like to thank:

Carol Rockwell who came through
with sewing assistance when I needed it most.

Ellen Pahl, technical editor, who was meticulous.

All the Martingale & Company staff who made this book possible.

American Jane's Quilts for All Seasons
. . . and Some for No Reason
© 2008 by Sandy Klop

That Patchwork Place® is an imprint
of Martingale & Company®.

Martingale & Company
20205 144th Ave. NE
Woodinville, WA 98072-8478 USA
www.martingale-pub.com

Printed in China
13 12 11 10 09 08   8 7 6 5 4 3 2 1

**Library of Congress
Cataloging-in-Publication Data
is available upon request.**

ISBN: 978-1-56477-852-9

Mission Statement
Dedicated to providing quality products
and service to inspire creativity.

Credits
President & CEO: Tom Wierzbicki
Publisher: Jane Hamada
Editorial Director: Mary V. Green
Managing Editor: Tina Cook
Developmental Editor: Karen Costello Soltys
Technical Editor: Ellen Pahl
Copy Editor: Sheila Chapman Ryan
Design Director: Stan Green
Production Manager: Regina Girard
Illustrator: Laurel Strand
Cover & Text Designer: Regina Girard
Photographer: Brent Kane

Contents

✸ *Introduction* ✸

This book is divided into four sections reflecting the seasons of the year. It begins with summer and ends with spring. The quilts in each section loosely reflect the seasons—and I've also included some quilts for no other reason than fun.

The 14 projects vary in the skills required to make them; some are for beginning quilters, some are for experienced quilters, and some are challenging quilts for more advanced quilters. And they cover a range of subjects and techniques, with both piecing and appliqué methods. There are whimsical quilts such as "Dancing Ladies" (page 91) and romantic quilts such as "Be Mine" (page 65). There are fun-to-make quilts like

"Puppy Parade" (page 78) and "Whirligigs" (page 17), as well as puzzle quilts like "Tessellation" (page 45) and "Fiesta Wear" (page 22). You'll find color-saturated quilts like "Apple Crisp" (page 42) and "Magic Carpet" (page 39), and you can even reach for the stars with "All Stars" (page 70).

In addition to celebrating the seasons, these quilts can add coziness to your home and art to your walls. They celebrate events, give comfort to those suffering loss or illness, express gratitude, and raise money for multiple causes. So make a quilt for yourself, your family, a friend, a teacher, a school auction, or for no reason—just because you can.

Basic Quiltmaking

In this section, I've provided a brief overview of the quiltmaking process, along with specific techniques you'll need for making the quilts in this book. I'm assuming that you have basic skills and knowledge of rotary-cutting techniques. If you don't, I encourage you to take a class for beginners and check out some of the many wonderful books with detailed information for those who are just starting out.

Fabric Selection

I love scrappy quilts, and for me it's harder to pick 3 to 5 fabulous fabrics for one quilt than it is to pick 25 to 85 fabrics! The more fabrics you have, the more they work—or rather "play"—together. The ones that don't get along will let you know right away.

If you are really stuck for a color scheme, choose a multicolored print fabric that you like, and then use the dots along the selvage or the colors in the print as your companion colors. You may or may not end up using the initial fabric, but it will direct you to others.

Audition fabrics with the ones you've already selected and they will either look comfortable with the others, or they will "jump out" as not belonging. If you're undecided about a particular one, take it out and see if you miss it when it's gone.

Staying Organized

When I worked in a fabric store, my favorite part was cutting the fabrics a customer had chosen, then folding them neatly and lining them up so we could see how great they looked together. I still love to cut all the pieces for a quilt first and then stack them neatly in a box so they are ready to go. I did this with "Tessellation" (page 45). I like to see all my choices when planning the next block. A friend of mine uses a laundry drying rack to hold multiple strips in sequence near her sewing station. That would be a great way to stay organized for the "All Stars" quilt (page 70) or "Fiesta Wear" (page 22). Determine a method of organization that works best for you.

The Keys to Accurate Piecing

There are many variables that come into play when piecing a quilt together. The first is accurate cutting. I'm amazed when I look at old quilts and remember they didn't have rotary cutters. Learning to use a mat, ruler, and rotary cutter is essential for today's quilter. The more accurate you are from the beginning, the more satisfaction you will have as you proceed.

The second most important variable is sewing an accurate ¼" seam. A good way to check is to sew two 1½" strips together and then measure to check whether the resulting strip is 2½" wide. If it's not, make adjustments until it is exact. Try sewing on ¼" graph paper to see where the fabric edge should be in relation to your presser foot. Many quilters make a guide with several layers of masking tape on the bed of their sewing machine.

The third most important variable is pressing. Usually, you will press toward the darker fabric after setting the seam flat (pressing it as it was sewn). There are times when you'll want to press toward the lighter fabric, however, to help you lock seams together for a tight intersection. Be sure to press the seams of strip sets completely flat. Any folds or pleats at the seams will reduce your accuracy when subcutting the strip sets. Exercise caution when pressing pieces with bias edges; stretching and distortion can easily occur.

Strip Sets

Strip sets are a very efficient way to get a lot of small pieces sewn together with ease. When making a checkerboard, it would be tedious if you had to cut all the light and dark squares and sew them all together in an alternating pattern. Instead, sew a light strip to a dark strip with one long seam, cut it to the size you need, and you have pairs in no time. Sew three strips together and stitching Nine Patch blocks is a snap, like the ones in "Dancing Ladies" (page 91).

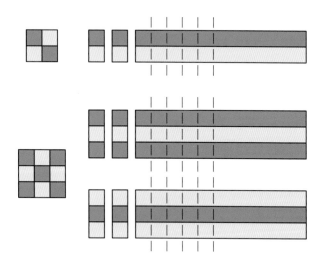

Strip sets can get more interesting when you have multiple rows in sequences as in "Fiesta Wear" (page 22), or when you cut the strip sets at an angle as in "All Stars" (page 70).

Angled Cuts

With rotary cutters and accurate rulers marked with various angle lines, angled cuts are a breeze. For making stars, I have found that a 60° angle is easier to work with than a 45° angle, because six points come together more easily than eight. When cutting angles from strip sets, keep the angle line that's marked on the ruler aligned with the edge of the fabric or on a seam line in your strip set. A 45° angle is often used in half-square-triangle units, quarter-square-triangle units, and also for mitered corners. (For more on mitered borders, see page 8.)

1. To cut a strip or strip set at a 60° angle, place the strip on your cutting mat. Align the 60° line of the ruler with the straight edge of the strip or a seam line in your strip set. Cut along the edge of the ruler with your rotary cutter.

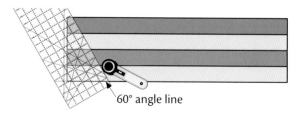

60° angle line

2. Discard the end piece. You now have a nice angled edge to begin cutting. Align the width of the piece you need, as instructed in the project, and make the cut along the edge of the ruler. The diagram shows the ruler aligned to cut a 2½" segment.

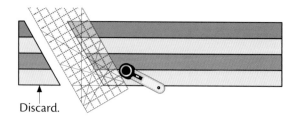

Discard.

You can cut a 45° or 30° cut in the same manner by aligning that line of the ruler with the strip or strip set.

The Rule of Y Seams

Y seams is another name for set-in seams. Don't let these seams scare you. Just follow the Y-seams rule: stop just before you sew into the seam allowance. Of course, that requires that you know exactly where the seam allowance begins. When you're in doubt, especially when sewing odd-angle pieces, draw in the ¼" seam allowance on your piece or template. Then mark where the seams intersect. You'll find Y seams in mitered borders and in the star quilts that incorporate 60° diamonds.

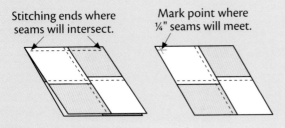

Stitching ends where seams will intersect.

Mark point where ¼" seams will meet.

Appliqué Techniques

I like to do appliqué by machine with either fusible web or fusible interfacing. Once fused to the background fabric, it's a snap to stitch around each piece. Use a stitch of your choice—zigzag, satin, blanket, or other decorative stitch—and sew with a matching thread color on top and a neutral thread color in the bobbin.

Fusible Appliqué

Always follow the manufacturer's instructions for the fusible web that you are using. I prefer a lightweight fusible-web product. It comes on a bolt by the yard and is typically 17" wide. Follow these general guidelines.

1. Trace all the pattern pieces for each fabric in a group on the paper side of the fusible web. The patterns are printed in reverse for easy tracing when doing fusible appliqué.

2. Iron the fusible web to the wrong side of the chosen fabric.

3. Cut out each pattern on the traced line and remove the paper backing.

4. Position the appliqué shape on the background fabric and iron in place. Now it's ready to stitch.

Interfacing Appliqué

This method is nice for larger shapes with gradual curves, such as circles or hearts. Fusible interfacing comes by the yard and is usually 23" wide. Choose a lightweight product and follow the manufacturer's instructions for fusing.

1. Trace the appliqué template onto the smooth side of the fusible interfacing. Your tracing will be the stitching line, so allow for a ¼" seam allowance all around. I like to use a ballpoint pen for tracing. It shows up well and the point rolls nicely on the interfacing.

2. Place the interfacing on your chosen fabric, with the fusible side on the right side of the fabric. Pin to hold the layers together.

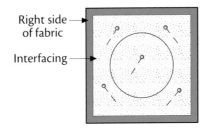

Right side of fabric

Interfacing

3. Sew on the drawn line. Cut out the shape ¼" away from the stitching line.

4. Make a small slit in the interfacing and turn right side out. Use a blunt tool such as a pen, chopstick, or crochet hook to smooth out the seams.

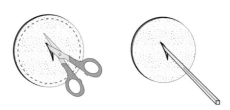

5. Position on the background fabric and fuse in place. Stitch by machine as desired.

Mitered Borders

I like the look of mitered borders, and they're not hard to add. The project instructions tell you how long to cut the border strips for mitering.

1. Find the center of a border strip and the center of one side of the quilt. Pin the border in place, matching center points. Begin and end sewing ¼" from the ends of the quilt top. Repeat for all four borders.

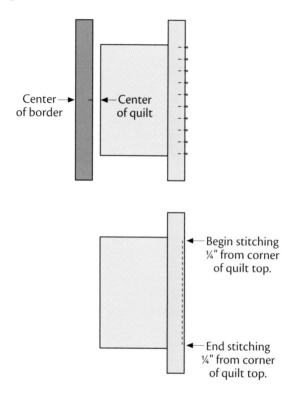

Center of border → ← Center of quilt

← Begin stitching ¼" from corner of quilt top.

← End stitching ¼" from corner of quilt top.

2. If your quilt has multiple mitered borders, sew the border strips together as one unit before pinning and sewing to your quilt. Fold the quilt wrong sides together at one corner and align the raw edges of the quilt. The borders should be right sides together, not pressed open. For quilts with multiple borders, line up the borders so that like-colored strips are aligned and pin to hold in place.

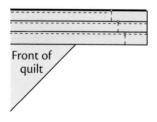

Front of quilt

3. Position your ruler so that the 45° line is on the stitching line of the border and the ¼" mark is exactly at the end of the stitching line. Cut the diagonal edge of the borders and then stitch a ¼" seam. Press the seam allowance open. Repeat for the remaining three corners.

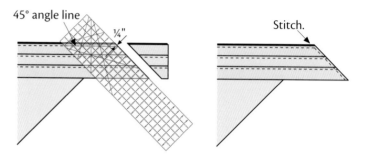

45° angle line   ¼"   Stitch.

Layering, Basting, and Quilting

Cut and piece the backing so that it is 2" to 4" larger than the quilt top. If you will be doing the quilting yourself, you will need to baste the layers together. To do this, tape the backing to a large flat surface, wrong side up. Layer the batting on top then add the quilt top, right side up. Pin or hand baste the three layers together approximately every 6". Hand or machine quilt as desired. If someone else is quilting it for you, check to see if they want the layers basted together.

Binding

Binding is the *ta-dah* of quilt making—you're finally finished! I most often cut binding strips 2¼" wide. If I'm using a heavy batting or working with flannels, I cut the binding strips 2½" to 2¾" wide.

1. Join all the strips together with diagonal seams. Press the seam allowances open as shown.

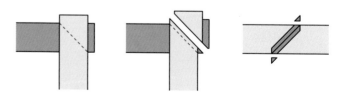

2. Fold the strip in half lengthwise with wrong sides together and press.

3. Align the raw edges along one side of the quilt and begin sewing 6" to 8" from the end of the binding strip. Stop sewing ¼" from the quilt's corner edge.

4. Take the quilt out of the machine and turn it to sew the next side. Fold the binding strip straight up, then back down along the new edge, with the short fold even with the edge of the quilt you just sewed. Begin sewing again down the next side, stopping ¼" from the next corner. Repeat the mitering at each corner around the quilt until you are 12" away from where you started.

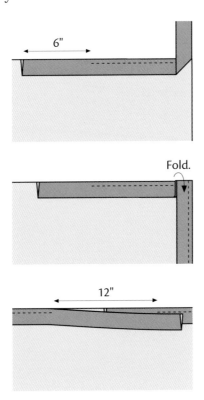

Fold.

5. Cut ½" off the beginning edge of your binding strip. This is usually selvage.

6. Take the end of your binding strip and lay it over the beginning edge in place along your quilt. Open up the ½" selvage that you just cut off and use it as a measuring gauge. Overlap the two ends of the binding by the length of the piece of selvage. This will be equal to the width that you cut your binding. If you cut your binding 2¼", it will be 2¼". If you cut it wider, it will be wider. Trim the binding at this point.

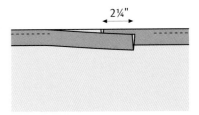

Overlap ends by width
of cut binding.

7. Pull both binding tails out to the side. Place them right sides together and sew them on the diagonal. Now, they will be just the right size to finish sewing by machine. Trim the seam allowance and finish sewing the binding to the quilt.

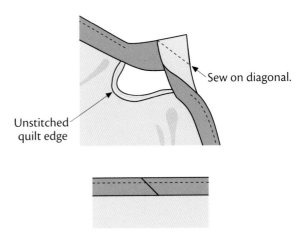

Sew on diagonal.

Unstitched
quilt edge

8. Turn the folded edge of the binding over to the back and hand stitch it to just cover the seam line.

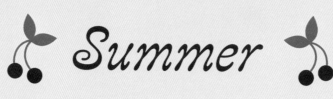

Summer

On a summer day, I could rise with the chickens, gather the eggs, tend the garden, and make some pies for dinner. In the afternoon I could sit on the porch, sip lemonade, and then read a good book. In the evening I could have a potluck picnic with friends and neighbors, and then stargaze as the world goes to sleep.
No, I think I'd rather make a quilt.

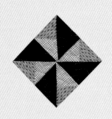

Star Diamond

Skill level: Intermediate

Finished quilt: 70" x 74½"

Finished block: 13⅞" x 12"

Materials

Yardages are based on 42"-wide fabrics.

3 yards *total* of assorted light taupe prints for setting triangles, borders 1 and 5, and binding

2½ yards *total* of assorted red, white, blue, and gold fabrics for Star Diamond blocks (**or** 20 fat eighths or ⅛-yard cuts)

2⅛ yards of white print for block background

½ yard of navy print for border 2

½ yard of cream print for border 3

½ yard of red print for border 4

4½ yards of fabric for backing

74" x 79" piece of batting

Cutting

All measurements include a ¼"-wide seam allowance.

From the assorted taupe prints, cut:

6 strips, 6¾" x 42"*

8 strips, 1¾" x 42"

8 strips, 3" x 42"

8 binding strips, 2¼" x 42"

From the assorted red, white, blue, and gold fabrics, cut a *total* of:

40 strips, 2" x 42"

From the white print, cut:

20 strips, 3½" x 42"

From the navy print, cut:

8 strips, 1½" x 42"

From the cream print, cut:

8 strips, 1¾" x 42"

From the red print, cut:

8 strips, 1½" x 42"

*Strips can be of random lengths. You will need enough to equal at least 6 strips, 42" long.

Stargazing on clear summer nights is one of my favorite pastimes. The distant suns in the night sky seem to appear and disappear. I tried to mimic that in this quilt in which some of the stars loom large while others appear small, depending on the fabric choices.

Making the Star Diamond Blocks

You will need 18 blocks and 4 half blocks (with four star points).

1. For one block, select three fabrics from the assorted 2" strips. You will need one strip of the first fabric, two strips of the second fabric, and one strip of the third fabric. Sew the strips together into two pairs: one pair of fabrics 1 and 2 and one pair of fabrics 2 and 3. Press the seam allowances toward fabric 2.

2. Trim one end of the strip sets at a 60° angle, referring to "Angled Cuts" (page 6). Subcut each strip set into six segments, 2" wide. Save the remainder of the strip sets for making other blocks. You can mix and match the strip-set segments within the blocks as I did in my quilt. Some of the stars are made of three different fabrics and others have four.

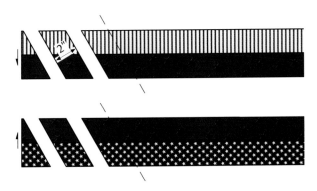

3. Sew the segments together in pairs (one from each strip set) to form six diamonds for the star points. When aligning the segments for sewing, match the center seams and pin if desired. The points will be offset by ¼".

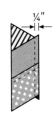

Make 6.

4. Sew the star points together in pairs, beginning and ending the stitching at the point where the ¼" seams will intersect. Refer to "The Rule of Y Seams" (page 7).

Accurate Set-In Seams

Notice that stopping the seam ¼" from the edges is not ¼" from the tip of the diamond. Stop where the seam intersects. Mark your pieces if necessary.

5. Continue in the same manner to join all six star points together. Press the seam allowances in a counterclockwise direction from the wrong side. The seam allowances will create a small star in the center of the block.

Star assembly

6. Trim the selvage ends of the 3½"-wide white background strips at a 60° angle. Then subcut each strip into six 3½"-wide segments.

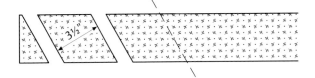

7. Sew the white background diamonds around the star, beginning ¼" from the outer edge and stopping ¼" from the inner point (which I call the "valley"). Press away from the center.

Sewing the Diamond Tips

The white background diamond is the same size as the pieced diamond for the star points. Align the first diamond on a star point and sew from the outside tip along the right-hand side and stop at the ¼" seam.

This should match the valley seam of the star. Repeat around the star with each diamond. Next, pivot the diamond to align with the adjacent, unsewn star point. Sew from the valley to the star point, stopping at the ¼" seam. Continue around the star.

8. Repeat steps 1–7 to complete 18 stars. To make the four half blocks for the sides, assemble four star points and sew them together with three light background diamonds. These partial blocks will be trimmed after the rows are assembled.

Make 18.

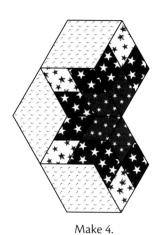

Make 4.

Adding the Setting Triangles

All blocks are joined with equilateral triangles.

1. Make a plastic template for the setting triangle and side setting triangle using the patterns (page 16). Use the templates to mark and cut 34 setting triangles and 12 side triangles from the 6¾"-wide taupe strips.

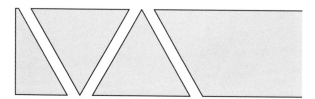

2. Arrange the blocks in five rows as shown in the quilt assembly diagram. Sew two side setting triangles to the left of the first star in the top row and one setting triangle on the upper-right side. Press the seam allowances toward the setting triangles.

3. Sew setting triangles on the lower-left side and upper-right side of the next star. Join to the first star with one diagonal seam. Continue across the row until the last star, adding two side triangles on the right.

4. Rows 2 and 4 begin and end with half stars. Sew one setting triangle to the upper right of the first half star in each row and one to the lower left of the last half star. Then complete the rows, joining the other three stars as you did for the previous rows.

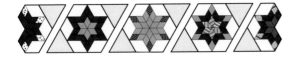

5. Sew the rows together and trim the half stars in rows 2 and 4 even with the side triangles.

Making the Mitered Borders

There are five borders on this quilt. The first and fifth are pieced from scraps of the assorted taupe prints. The middle three are pieced from 42"-long strips.

1. Sew two red, two off-white, and two navy 42"-long strips together end to end. Repeat to make four of these long strips (approximately 80" long) for each color.

2. For the inner border, piece the 1¾" taupe strips end to end to equal approximately 80". Make four. Repeat using the 3"-wide taupe strips for the outer border.

3. For each side of the quilt, sew all five borders together in the following sequence: narrow taupe strip, navy strip, cream strip, red strip, and wide taupe strip. Press all seam allowances toward the outer border.

Make 4.

4. Referring to "Mitered Borders" (page 8), sew the borders to the quilt.

Finishing the Quilt

1. Press the quilt top carefully and mark it for quilting.

2. Layer the quilt top with the backing and batting. Baste with thread for hand quilting or with safety pins for machine quilting.

3. Quilt as desired and bind with the 2¼"-wide taupe binding strips.

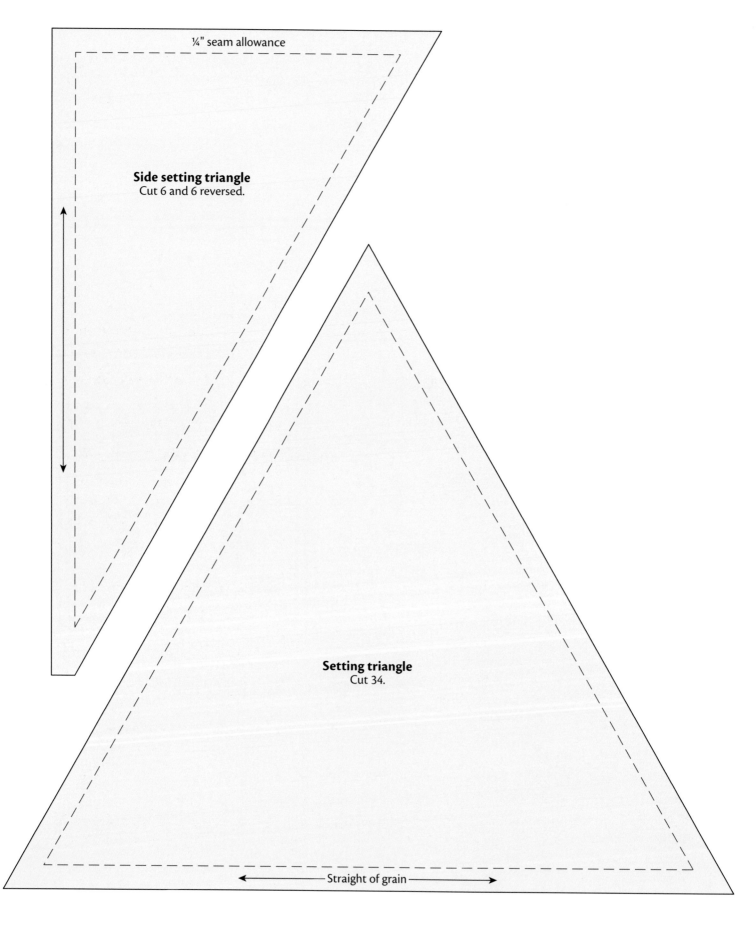

¼" seam allowance

Side setting triangle
Cut 6 and 6 reversed.

Setting triangle
Cut 34.

Straight of grain

Whirligigs

Materials

Yardages are based on 42"-wide fabrics.

⅜ yard *each* of 8 assorted light red and light blue fabrics for setting pieces (squares, rectangles, and triangles)

2 yards of light blue plaid for outer border

9 fat eighths of assorted light, medium, and dark red prints and striped fabrics for pinwheels and sawtooth border

9 fat eighths of assorted light, medium, and dark blue prints and striped fabrics for pinwheels and sawtooth border

4 yards of fabric for backing

½ yard of fabric for binding

67" x 67" piece of batting

Cutting

The cutting goes quickly if you layer your fabrics and cut multiple squares at a time. When you are cutting stripes, cut for two blocks at a time so that you can select four pieces with the stripes going in the same direction for each block. The cut pieces are similar in size, so to avoid confusion, I suggest that you cut and piece the 8" blocks first. Then go on to the 6", and then the 4" blocks. Label the triangles as indicated in the cutting instructions. All measurements include a ¼"-wide seam allowance.

8" Pinwheels

From the medium and dark red and medium and dark blue fat eighths, cut:

16 squares, 4⅞" x 4⅞"; cut each square once diagonally to yield 32 triangles and label A*

From the light red and light blue fat eighths, cut:

8 squares, 5¼" x 5¼"; cut each square twice diagonally to yield 32 triangles and label B

From the medium red and medium blue fat eighths, cut:

8 squares, 5¼" x 5¼"; cut each square twice diagonally to yield 32 triangles and label B

6" Pinwheels

From the medium and dark red and medium and dark blue fat eighths, cut:

28 squares, 3⅞" x 3⅞"; cut each square once diagonally to yield 56 triangles and label C*

From the light red and light blue fat eighths, cut:

14 squares, 4¼" x 4¼"; cut each square twice diagonally to yield 56 triangles and label D

From the medium red and medium blue fat eighths, cut:

14 squares, 4¼" x 4¼"; cut each square twice diagonally to yield 56 triangles and label D

Cut the squares in pairs so that you will have matching triangles within the blocks.

The soft and faded red, white, and blue shades in this quilt speak of sunny summer days and warm evening breezes. Spinning whirligigs are ready for the parade without being overtly patriotic. The three different whirligig sizes create movement and combine neatly into 12" blocks.

4" Pinwheels

From the medium and dark red and medium and dark blue fat eighths, cut:

16 squares, $2\frac{7}{8}$" x $2\frac{7}{8}$"; cut each square once diagonally to yield 32 triangles and label E*

From the light red and light blue fat eighths, cut:

8 squares, $3\frac{1}{4}$" x $3\frac{1}{4}$"; cut each square twice diagonally to yield 32 triangles and label F

From the medium red and medium blue fat eighths, cut:

8 squares, $3\frac{1}{4}$" x $3\frac{1}{4}$"; cut each square twice diagonally to yield 32 triangles and label F

Setting Pieces

From assorted light red and light blue fabrics, cut:

6 squares, $9\frac{3}{4}$" x $9\frac{3}{4}$"; cut each square twice diagonally to yield 24 triangles

14 squares, $6\frac{1}{2}$" x $6\frac{1}{2}$"

16 rectangles, $4\frac{1}{2}$" x $8\frac{1}{2}$"

Borders

From scraps of the remaining dark and medium red and dark blue fat eighths, cut:

70 squares, $2\frac{3}{8}$" x $2\frac{3}{8}$"; cut each square once diagonally to yield 140 triangles

From scraps of the remaining medium and light red and light blue fat eighths, cut:

70 squares, $2\frac{3}{8}$" x $2\frac{3}{8}$"; cut each square once diagonally to yield 140 triangles

From the light blue plaid, cut on the *lengthwise* grain:

4 strips, $4\frac{1}{2}$" x 66"

Binding

From the binding fabric, cut:

7 strips, $2\frac{1}{4}$" x 42"

Cut the squares in pairs so that you will have matching triangles within the blocks.

Making the Whirligig Blocks

You will be making Whirligig blocks in three different finished sizes: 8", 6", and 4". They are all assembled the same way and go together quickly, regardless of the finished size.

1. Choose the three fabrics that you want to go together in one block: select four matching A triangles, four matching light B triangles, and four matching medium B triangles. Sew the B triangles together in pairs. Press toward the darker fabric. Make four.

Make 4.

2. Sew the B units from step 1 to the dark A triangles. Press toward A. Join the units as shown to make a Pinwheel block. Repeat to make eight 8" blocks.

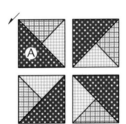

8" pinwheel.
Make 8.

3. Repeat steps 1 and 2 to make fourteen 6" Pinwheel blocks using the C and D triangles and eight 4" blocks using the E and F triangles. Note that I made some of the 6" and 4" Pinwheel blocks spin in opposite directions. Five of the 6" blocks and two of the 4" blocks are made with the larger triangles in the opposite position within the blocks.

6" pinwheel.
Make 14.

4" pinwheel.
Make 8.

Assembling the Quilt Center

1. Sew eight of the 4½" x 8½" rectangles to the 8" Pinwheel blocks as shown. Press toward the rectangles.

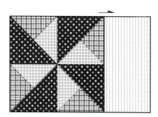

2. Sew the remaining eight 4½" x 8½" rectangles to the 4" Pinwheel blocks as shown. Press toward the rectangles.

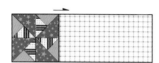

3. Join the units from steps 1 and 2 to make eight units. The units should measure 12½" x 12½".

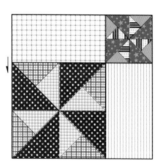

Make 8.

4. Make five four-patch units with the ten 6" Pinwheel blocks and ten 6½" squares as shown.

Make 5.

5. Sew each of the four remaining 6" pinwheels to two setting triangles as shown.

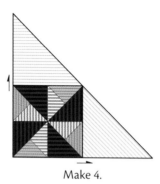

Make 4.

6. Sew the remaining 6½" squares to two setting triangles each.

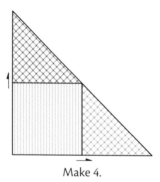

Make 4.

7. Sew two setting triangles together for each corner.

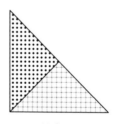

Make 4.

8. Arrange the blocks and setting pieces together in diagonal rows, referring to the quilt diagram. Sew the blocks and background pieces into rows. Sew the rows together, adding the corner triangles last.

Making and Adding Borders

1. Sew together the light, medium, and dark 2⅜" triangles to make 140 half-square-triangle units. Press toward the darker triangles.

Make 140.

2. Make a top and bottom border with 36 half-square-triangle units in each. Make side borders with 34 half-square-triangle units in each. Press the seam allowances all in one direction.

Side border.
Make 2.

Top/bottom border.
Make 2.

3. Sew the top and bottom borders to the quilt. Press toward the center of the quilt. Sew the side borders to the quilt; press.

Mitering the Outer Border

Refer to "Mitered Borders" (page 8) to add the light blue plaid outer border.

Finishing the Quilt

1. Press the quilt top carefully and mark it for quilting.

2. Layer the quilt top with the backing and batting. Baste with thread for hand quilting or with safety pins for machine quilting.

3. Quilt as desired and bind with the 2¼"-wide binding strips.

Fiesta Wear

Materials

Yardages are based on 42"-wide fabrics.

Assorted Prints

⅓ yard *each* of 6 prints for fabric 1

½ yard *each* of 6 prints for fabric 3

⅝ yard *each* of 6 prints for fabric 5

Assorted Solids

½ yard *each* of 6 solids for fabric 2

⅝ yard *each* of 6 solids for fabric 4

⅔ yard *each* of 6 solids for fabric 6

Additional Materials

3⅞ yards of black fabric for blocks and inner border (fabric 7)

9 yards of fabric for backing

⅞ yard of fabric for binding

102" x 102" piece of batting

Cutting

Cut strips as directed to make two blocks and one half block at a time. The instructions are written so that the solid and print fabrics alternate. Feel free to vary the placement as I did in many of the blocks. All measurements include a ¼"-wide seam allowance.

For *each* set of two blocks and one half block, cut:

From print fabric 1:

1 strip, 2" x 42"; cut in half to yield 2 half strips

From solid fabric 2:

2 strips, 2" x 42"; cut each strip in half to yield 4 half strips (1 is extra)

From print fabric 3:

2 strips, 2" x 42"; cut each strip in half to yield 4 half strips

From solid fabric 4:

3 strips, 2" x 42"; cut each strip in half to yield 6 half strips (1 is extra)

From print fabric 5:

3 strips, 2" x 42"; cut each strip in half to yield 6 half strips

From solid fabric 6:

4 strips, 2" x 42"; cut each strip in half to yield 8 half strips (1 is extra)

From the black fabric (fabric 7), cut:

54 strips, 2" x 42"; crosscut into 91 half strips, 2" x 21", and 169 squares, 2" x 2"

9 inner-border strips, 2" x 42"

Binding

From the binding fabric, cut:

11 strips, 2¼" x 42"

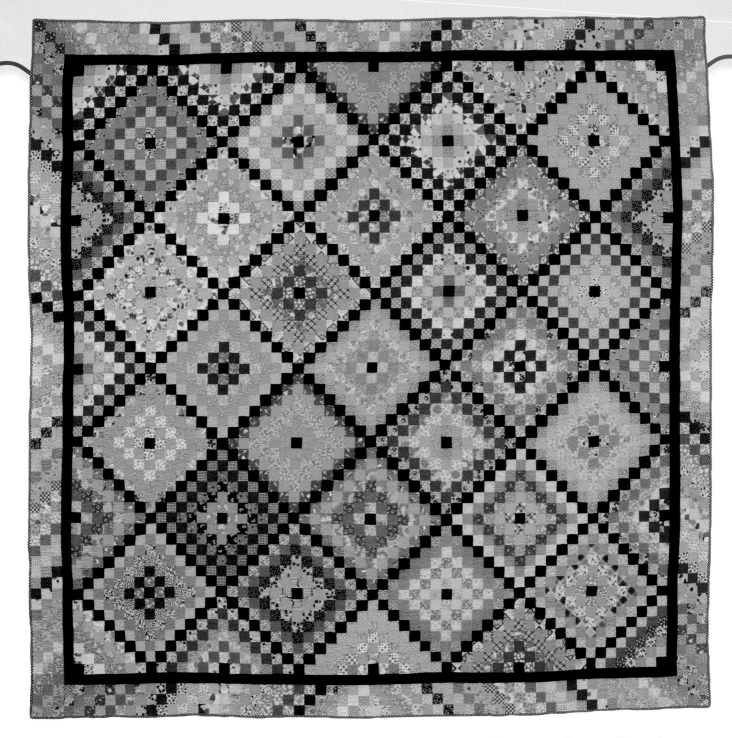

*Old quilts and little squares always get my attention, so when a friend
shared an antique quilt top with me, I had to try making my own version.
I hope you will too! The bright colors remind me of clothing worn in
countries south of the border. The blocks are constructed in pairs
based on strip sets. If you want each block to be different,
sew with a friend and trade blocks as you go.*

Making the Blocks

Make strip sets using fabrics 1–7 as directed below. Press the seam allowances in the direction shown on the diagrams. You will make two whole blocks and one half block from each group of seven fabrics. After you complete 12 half blocks for the sides of the quilt, make four quarter blocks for the corners.

1. Sew strips of fabrics 1–7 together to make the spacer rows. Make two of these strip sets and cut 11 segments, 2" wide. Set the remainder aside for use in other blocks or in the borders.

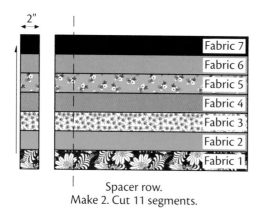

Spacer row.
Make 2. Cut 11 segments.

2. Sew strips of fabrics 2–7 together to make row 1. Cut 10 segments, 2" wide.

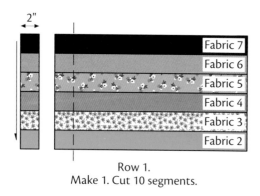

Row 1.
Make 1. Cut 10 segments.

3. Sew strips of fabrics 3–7 together to make row 2. Cut 10 segments, 2" wide.

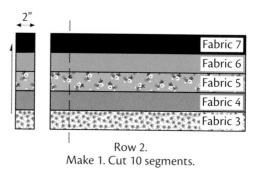

Row 2.
Make 1. Cut 10 segments.

4. Sew strips of fabrics 4–7 together to make row 3. Cut 10 segments, 2" wide.

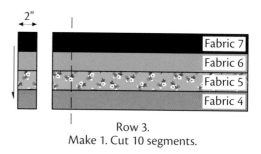

Row 3.
Make 1. Cut 10 segments.

5. Sew strips of fabrics 5–7 together to make row 4. Cut 10 segments, 2" wide.

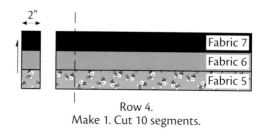

Row 4.
Make 1. Cut 10 segments.

6. Sew strips of fabrics 6–7 together to make row 5. Cut 10 segments, 2" wide.

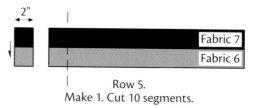

Row 5.
Make 1. Cut 10 segments.

7. Row 6 is a single 2" black square. Sew rows 1–6 together to make 10 triangle sections.

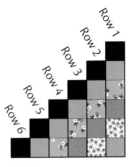

Make 10.

8. Sew four of the units from step 7 together with four spacer rows and one 2" black square to complete a block. Repeat to make another whole block.

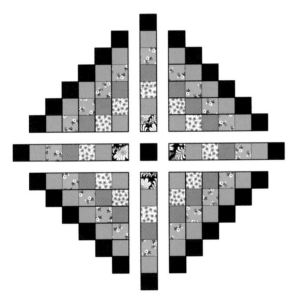

Block assembly

9. Sew two of the triangle units from step 7 with three spacer rows and one 2" black square to make one half block.

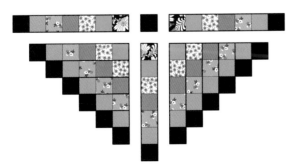

10. Repeat the cutting and piecing steps until you have 25 whole blocks, 12 half blocks, and 4 quarter blocks for the corners.

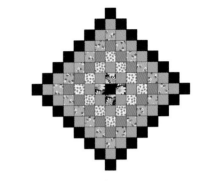

Make 25.

Make 12.   Make 4.

Assembling the Quilt Top

1. Arrange the blocks, half blocks, and quarter blocks together in diagonal rows.

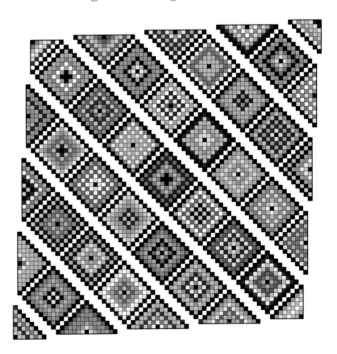

2. To join the blocks, match up the outside row of squares and sew a seam diagonally through the center of the squares. Trim off the excess, leaving a ¼" seam allowance. Sew the blocks into diagonal rows. Then sew the rows together.

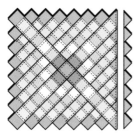

With rights sides together, sew seam through the diagonal. Trim, leaving ¼" seam allowance.

Pinning the Blocks

If you only concentrate on one intersection at a time, you can sew without pinning. I used one pin to spear the two corners and then moved it to the next two corners.

3. Piece together the nine 2" black strips to make two inner-border strips, 2" x 86", and two inner-border strips, 2" x 89".

4. Sew the shorter borders to the quilt sides, and then sew the longer borders to the top and bottom. Press toward the black borders.

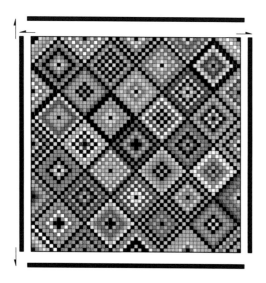

Making the Pieced Outer Border

The outer border is made from the remaining block fabrics and segments cut from the leftover strip sets. Work on a design wall to arrange the border segments as you go.

1. Remove the black strips from all the strip sets. Then separate the six strips into sets of three strips.

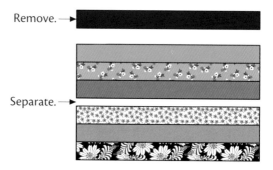

2. Cut 2"-wide segments from the strips and use the diagram as a guide to assemble the borders on your design wall. You may need to cut 2" x 21" strips from your remaining block fabrics to assemble additional strip sets. You'll need strip sets made of the same three fabrics as shown; or make them to coordinate with leftover segments.

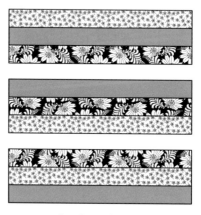

Border strip sets

3. Start in the center of each border and work outward, making sure the diagonals of color are going in the same direction to create the Vs. Arrange the strip segments and piece additional strip sets as necessary to create the pattern. You will need 29 segments on either side of the center. For the corners, sew nine-patch units, making sure the colors of the diagonals match the squares in the corners of the adjacent border section.

Make 2.   Make 4.   Make 4.   Make 4.   Make 2.

4. Sew the border segments together to create four long border strips. Add the corner blocks to the ends of the top and bottom borders.

5. Sew the borders without corner blocks to the sides of the quilt. Press toward the black inner border. Sew the remaining borders to the top and bottom. Press.

Finishing the Quilt

1. Press the quilt top carefully and mark it for quilting.

2. Layer the quilt top with the backing and batting. Baste with thread for hand quilting or with safety pins for machine quilting.

3. Quilt as desired and bind with the 2¼"-wide binding strips.

Chickens, Cherries, and Checks

Materials

Yardages are based on 42"-wide fabrics.

⅜ yard *each* of 4 assorted light fabrics for Cherry block backgrounds

5 fat quarters of assorted light fabrics for Chicken block backgrounds

5 fat quarters of assorted dark fabrics for chickens

¾ yard of dark fabric for checked outer border and binding

⅛ yard *each* of 4 red fabrics for cherries and checks

⅜ yard of light fabric for inner border

⅛ yard *each* of 3 green fabrics for stems, leaves, and nest

⅓ yard of light fabric for checked outer border

Scraps of assorted colors for chicken legs, feathers, combs, wattles, and beaks

2⅝ yards of fabric for backing

2 yards of lightweight fusible web

47" x 47" piece of batting

Cutting

All measurements include a ¼"-wide seam allowance.

From *each* of the 5 assorted light fat quarters for Chicken block backgrounds, cut:

1 square, 11¾" x 11¾" (5 total)

From *each* of the 4 assorted light fabrics for Cherry block backgrounds, cut:

1 strip, 1¾" x 42"; cut each strip into 1 strip, 1¾" x 30" (4 total), and 2 squares, 1¾" x 1¾" (8 total)

1 square, 9¼" x 9¼" (4 total)

From *each* of the 4 red fabrics, cut:

1 strip, 1¾" x 42; cut each strip into 1 strip, 1¾" x 30" (4 total), and 2 squares, 1¾" x 1¾" (8 total)

From the light fabric for inner border, cut:

2 strips, 2⅝" x 34¼"

2 strips, 2⅝" x 38½"

From the light fabric for checked outer border, cut:

3 strips, 2½" x 42"

2 squares, 2½" x 2½"

From the dark fabric for checked outer border and binding, cut:

3 strips, 2½" x 42"

2 squares, 2½" x 2½"

5 binding strips, 2¼" x 42"

There is nothing more country than chickens, cherries, and checks. Spice up your kitchen with this farm-fresh look. You'll have a little bit of summer inside all year long.

Making the Appliqué Blocks

The appliqué for this quilt was done with fusible web, so the pattern pieces are reversed. However, you can use the appliqué method of your choice. Refer to "Fusible Appliqué" (page 7) as needed.

1. Trace all the chicken patterns (pages 32–37) onto the paper side of the fusible web. Cut out each piece approximately ¼" outside the traced lines.

2. Iron the shapes to the wrong side of the appropriate fabrics following the manufacturer's instructions. Polka dots work great for the eyes.

3. Cut out each appliqué shape along the lines, peel off the paper backing, and place on the 11¾" background squares. Use the photo (page 29) for placement guidance.

4. Fuse in place with your iron following the manufacturer's instructions. Stitch around each piece using a machine-appliqué stitch and matching thread. The bobbin thread can be a neutral color because it will not show. The nest for the center block will be appliquéd later, after the blocks are assembled.

5. Repeat steps 1–4 to appliqué the four Cherry blocks using the patterns (page 37). Group all cherries, stems, and leaves together when tracing, and then fuse to the appropriate fabric. Fuse the designs to the 9¼" background squares.

Making the Block Borders

1. For each Cherry block, make a strip set using the 1¾" x 30" background strip that matches the block background and a 1¾" x 30" red strip. Press toward the red strips and crosscut each strip set into 14 segments, 1¾" wide.

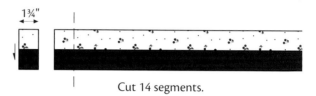

Cut 14 segments.

2. Join the segments together, adding the two matching red and two matching 1¾" light squares. Add the borders to the Cherry blocks as shown. Sew the side borders first, and then the top and bottom borders.

Chicken A

Chicken B

Chicken C

Chicken D

Chicken E

Joining the Blocks

1. Arrange the blocks, alternating Chicken and Cherry blocks. Sew the blocks into rows. Press the seam allowances toward the Chicken blocks. Sew the rows together.

2. Appliqué the nest to the center Chicken block.

Adding the Borders

1. Sew the 2⅝" x 34¼" inner-border strips to the sides of the quilt. Press toward the inner border. Sew the 2⅝" x 38½" inner-border strips to the top and bottom; press.

2. For the checked outer border, make three strip sets using the 2½" x 42" light and dark strips. Crosscut the strip sets into 38 segments, 2½" wide.

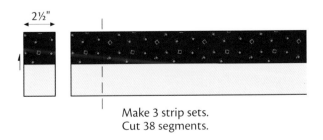

2½"

Make 3 strip sets.
Cut 38 segments.

3. Sew the border strips as shown. Use the additional 2½" light and dark squares as needed to form the border strips.

4. Sew the side borders first, then the top and bottom borders.

Finishing the Quilt

It's not a quilt until it's quilted! I stipple quilted all but the appliqué pieces. Bind it quick and hang it in your kitchen.

1. Press the quilt top carefully and mark it for quilting.

2. Layer the quilt top with the backing and batting. Baste with thread for hand quilting or with safety pins for machine quilting.

3. Quilt as desired and bind with the 2¼"-wide binding strips.

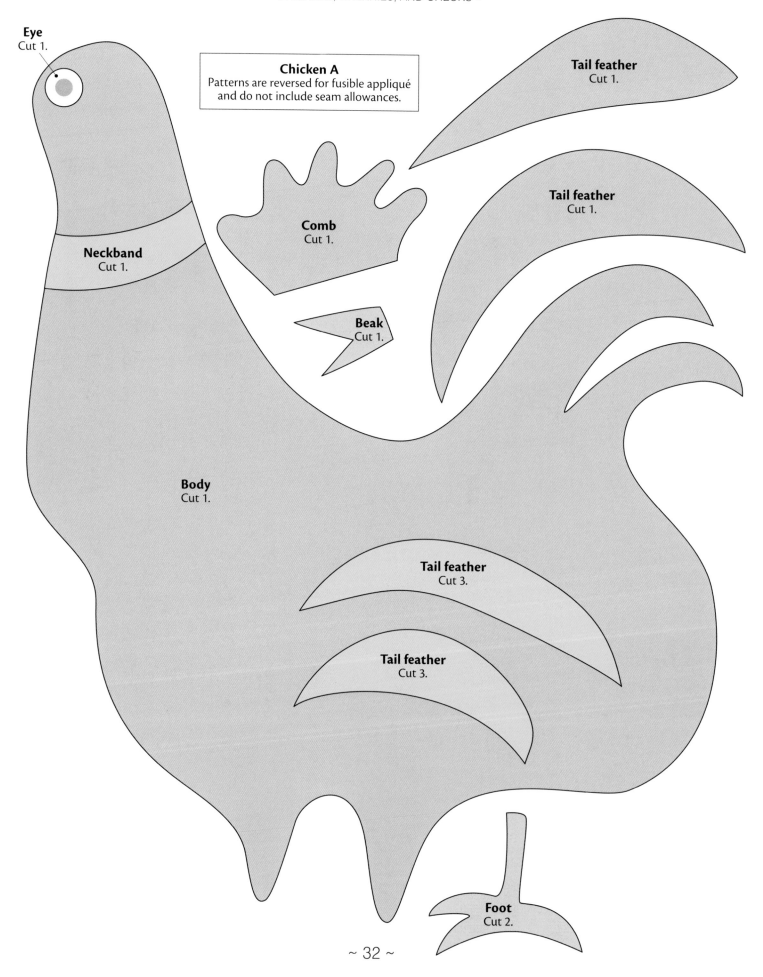

Eye
Cut 1.

Chicken A
Patterns are reversed for fusible appliqué
and do not include seam allowances.

Tail feather
Cut 1.

Comb
Cut 1.

Tail feather
Cut 1.

Neckband
Cut 1.

Beak
Cut 1.

Body
Cut 1.

Tail feather
Cut 3.

Tail feather
Cut 3.

Foot
Cut 2.

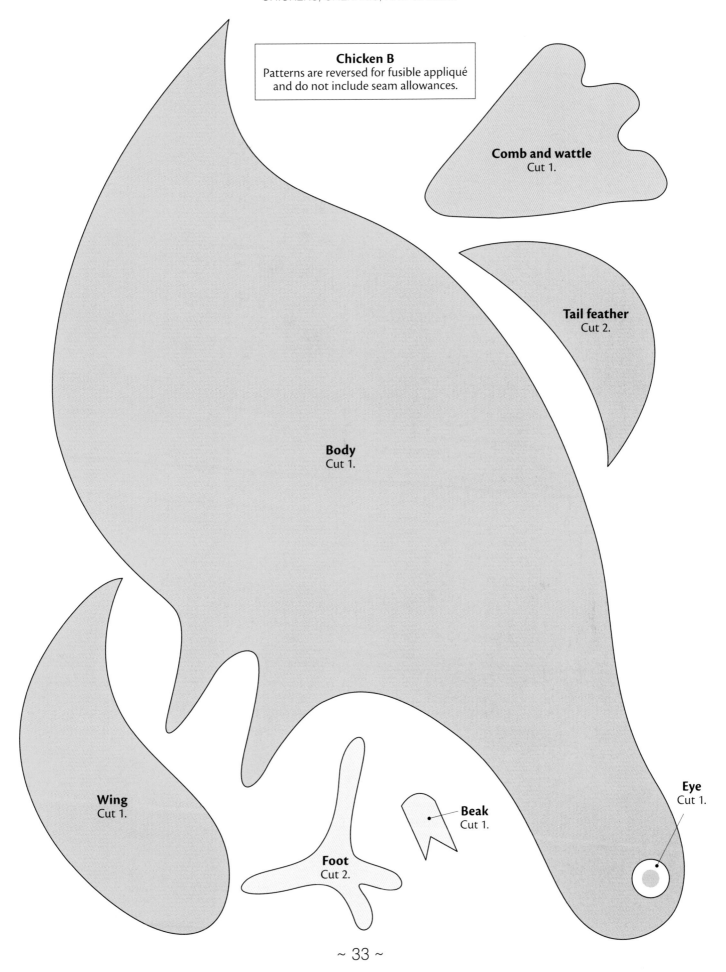

Chicken B
Patterns are reversed for fusible appliqué and do not include seam allowances.

Comb and wattle
Cut 1.

Tail feather
Cut 2.

Body
Cut 1.

Wing
Cut 1.

Foot
Cut 2.

Beak
Cut 1.

Eye
Cut 1.

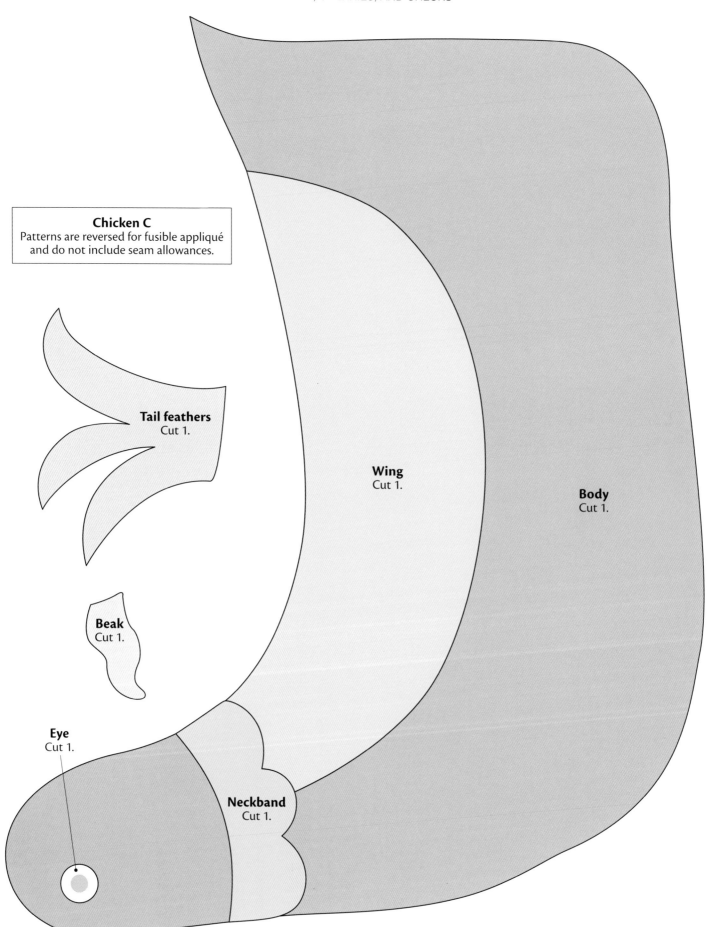

Chicken C
Patterns are reversed for fusible appliqué
and do not include seam allowances.

Tail feathers
Cut 1.

Wing
Cut 1.

Body
Cut 1.

Beak
Cut 1.

Eye
Cut 1.

Neckband
Cut 1.

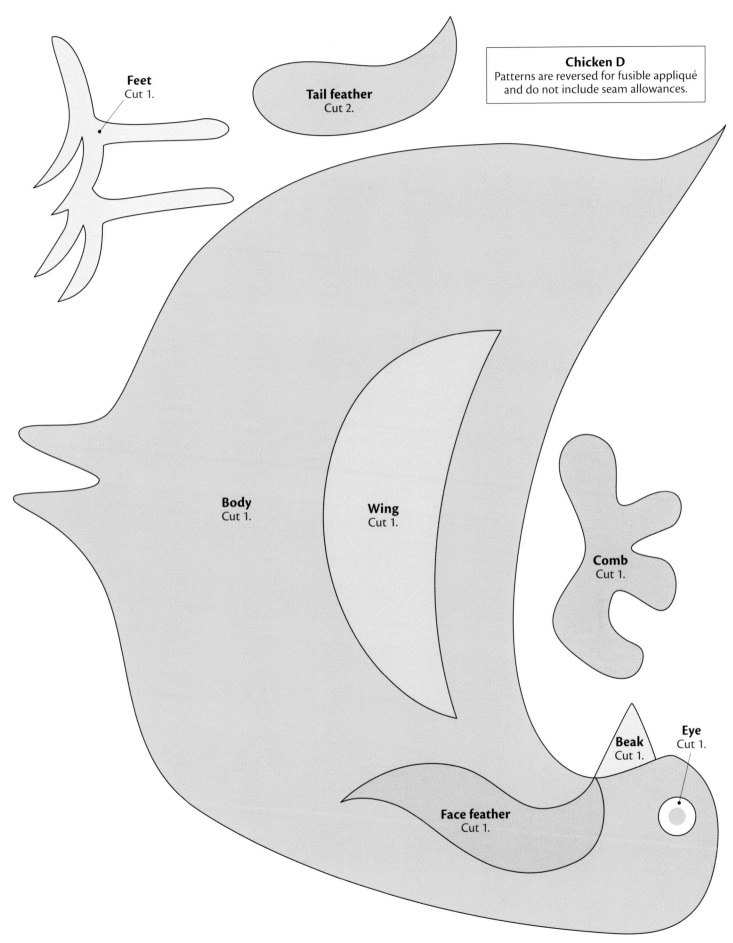

Feet
Cut 1.

Tail feather
Cut 2.

Chicken D
Patterns are reversed for fusible appliqué
and do not include seam allowances.

Body
Cut 1.

Wing
Cut 1.

Comb
Cut 1.

Beak
Cut 1.

Eye
Cut 1.

Face feather
Cut 1.

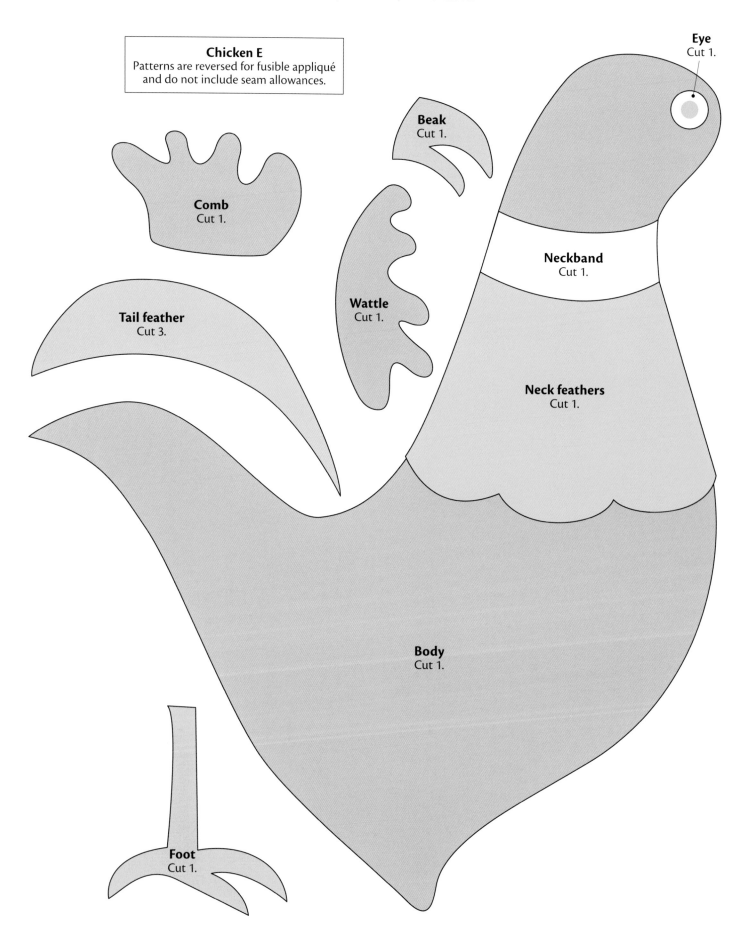

Chicken E
Patterns are reversed for fusible appliqué
and do not include seam allowances.

Eye
Cut 1.

Beak
Cut 1.

Comb
Cut 1.

Neckband
Cut 1.

Wattle
Cut 1.

Tail feather
Cut 3.

Neck feathers
Cut 1.

Body
Cut 1.

Foot
Cut 1.

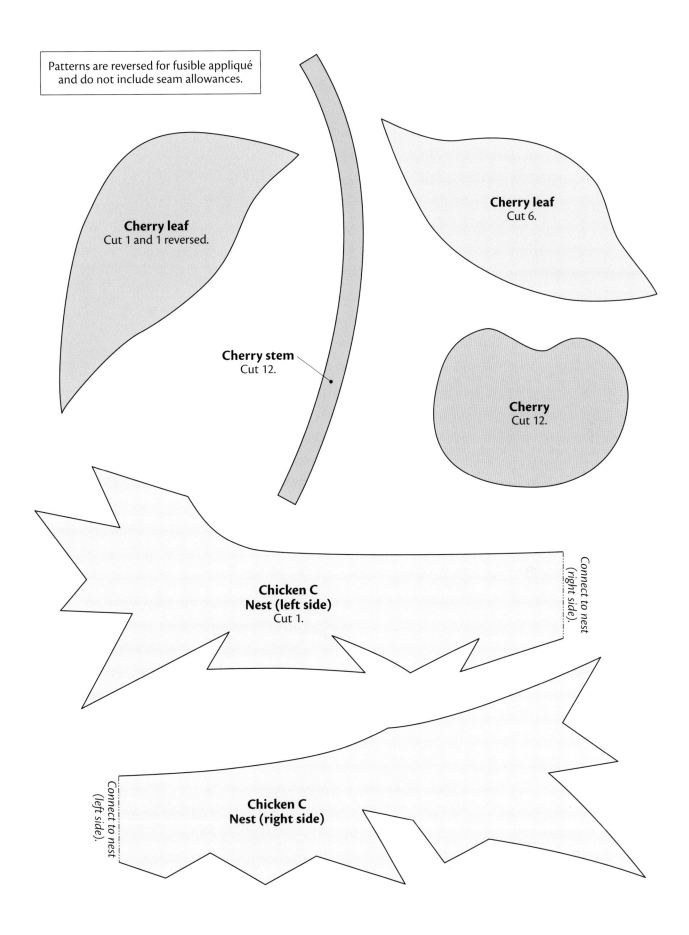

Patterns are reversed for fusible appliqué and do not include seam allowances.

Cherry leaf
Cut 1 and 1 reversed.

Cherry leaf
Cut 6.

Cherry stem
Cut 12.

Cherry
Cut 12.

**Chicken C
Nest (left side)**
Cut 1.

*Connect to nest
(right side).*

*Connect to nest
(left side).*

**Chicken C
Nest (right side)**

Fall

On a perfect fall day, I could go for a long walk through the crunchy dry leaves, or maybe gather some acorns and buy a pumpkin. Then I could make a hearty vegetable soup, bake bread, and make an apple crisp for dessert. In the evening I could light a fire, curl up under a quilt, and watch a movie. But I'd rather make a quilt.

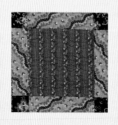

Magic Carpet

Skill level: Beginner

Finished quilt: 72½" x 72½"

Finished block: 12" x 12"

Materials

Yardages are based on 42"-wide fabrics.

⅜ yard *each* of 18 assorted indienne* chintz and calico fabrics

4½ yards of fabric for backing

⅝ yard of fabric for binding

77" x 77" piece of batting

Originally this was a general term referring to printed cottons from India. It now refers to small-scale cotton prints that come from France.

Cutting

All measurements include a ¼"-wide seam allowance.

From *each* of the 18 assorted fabrics, cut:

1 strip, 8½" x 42"; cut each strip into
2 squares, 8½" x 8½" (36 total), and
8 rectangles, 2½" x 8½" (144 total)

1 strip, 2½" x 42"; cut into 8 squares,
2½" x 2½" (144 total)

From the binding fabric, cut:

8 strips, 2¼" x 42"

Making the Blocks

1. Choose three fabrics for a block. You will need one 8½" square, four matching 2½" x 8½" rectangles, and four matching 2½" squares.

2. Sew two rectangles to the sides of the 8½" square. Press toward the rectangles.

3. Sew a small square to each end of the remaining two rectangles. Press toward the rectangles. Sew these to the unit from step 2 to complete the block.

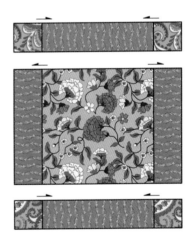

4. Repeat steps 1–3 to make 36 blocks.

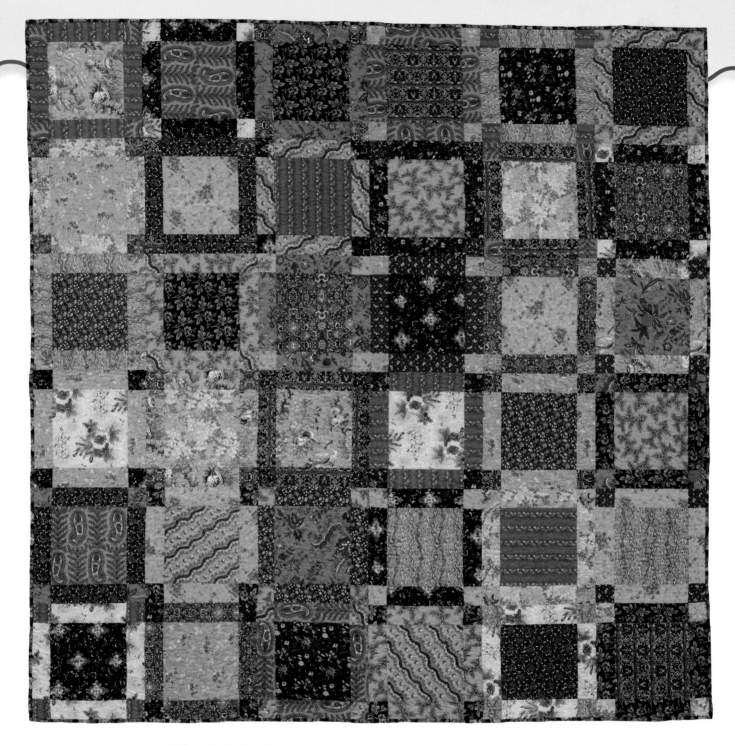

*The fabric choices for this quilt were inspired by
Persian carpets. The deep rich colors are reminiscent
of autumn flowers and lush harvests of fruits, berries,
and garden produce. The cutting and assembly
are so quick, it's like magic.*

Assembling the Quilt Top

1. Arrange the blocks on a design wall or a large piece of flannel. Rearrange until you are satisfied with the color placement.

Color Tip

Try not to place dominant or strong colors too close to each other.

2. Sew the blocks together in rows, pressing the seam allowances in opposite directions from row to row. Then sew the rows together and press the seam allowances in one direction.

Finishing the Quilt

1. Press the quilt top carefully and mark it for quilting.

2. Layer the quilt top with the backing and batting. Baste with thread for hand quilting or with safety pins for machine quilting.

3. Quilt as desired and bind with the 2¼"-wide binding strips.

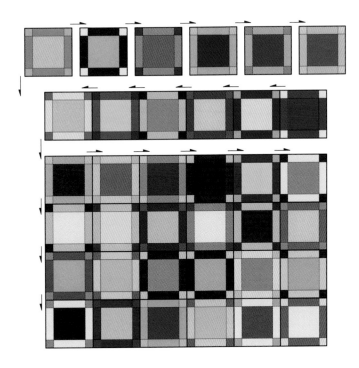

Apple Crisp

Skill level: Intermediate

Finished quilt: 77½" x 77½"

Finished block: 6½" x 6½"

Materials

Yardages are based on 42"-wide fabrics.

¼ yard *each* of 20 assorted light and medium prints

2½ yards of black polka-dot fabric for outer border*

¼ yard *each* of 6 assorted medium to dark solids (or prints that read as solids)

⅝ yard of red fabric for inner border

5 yards of fabric for backing

⅔ yard of fabric for binding

82" x 82" piece for batting

*Yardage is based on cutting borders on the lengthwise grain; 1½ yards of fabric is enough if you piece the outer border.

Cutting

All measurements include a ¼"-wide seam allowance.

From the assorted light and medium prints, cut a *total* of:

81 squares, 5" x 5"

5 squares, 7¾" x 7¾"; cut each square twice diagonally to yield 20 triangles

82 squares, 4⅛" x 4⅛"; cut each square once diagonally to yield 164 triangles*

4 squares, 3¾" x 3¾"

16 rectangles, 3¾" x 7"

From the assorted medium to dark solids (or prints that read as solids), cut a *total* of:

100 squares, 4⅛" x 4⅛"; cut each square once diagonally to yield 200 triangles**

From the red fabric, cut:

8 strips, 2" x 42"

From the black polka-dot fabric, cut on the *lengthwise* grain:

4 strips, 5" x 82"

From the binding fabric, cut:

9 strips, 2¼" x 42"

*Cut these in pairs so that you will have 4 matching triangles for each 5" center square.

**Cut these in matching groups of 4 so that you will have 8 matching triangles for each star.

Slice up your fabric for a simple one-block pattern that's as crisp as an apple. With just a little planning and easy piecing, you'll have a star-studded quilt for the crisp, clear, and cool fall nights.

Making Blocks and Quilt Center

For this quilt, you will need to work on a design wall. If you don't have a design wall, lay your blocks out on the floor. The center square of each star in the quilt is made of two different prints: a center square is surrounded by four matching print triangles. You will make these units first. Then arrange them on the design wall in rows to make the blocks and half blocks that will form the star points. The star points are made of the triangles cut from solid fabrics (or prints that read as solids). You will arrange them so that each star has eight matching star points.

Star Center block.
Make 41.

1. Sew a matching 4⅛" print triangle to each side of a 5" square. Press toward the triangles. Make 41 of these blocks.

2. Working in rows, lay out the pieces for the Star Point blocks and the half blocks. Row 1 begins and ends with a 3¾" square. Use the 3¾" x 7" rectangles, the triangles cut from solids, and the 7¾" triangles cut from prints. For row 2 you'll also make Star Point blocks in the same manner as the blocks in step 1. Follow the diagrams below to arrange triangles, rectangles and squares in rows so that the eight star points for each star will all be the same fabric.

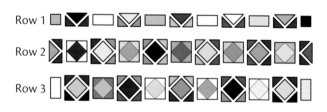

3. Assemble the Star Point blocks and half blocks as shown.

Star Point block.
Make 40.

Half block.
Make 20.

4. Assemble the blocks and units in rows to create the pattern.

5. Continue to lay out pieces, sew the units, and sew them into rows. Repeat the row 2 and 3 sequence until you have sewn 10 rows together. Then repeat row 1, but rotate the half blocks so that the star points are going in the correct direction.

Adding the Borders

1. Join the 2" x 42" red strips together in pairs to make four long strips.

2. Sew a red strip to each of the black polka-dot strips. Press toward black polka-dot strips.

3. Referring to "Mitered Borders" (page 8), sew the border units from step 2 to the quilt top.

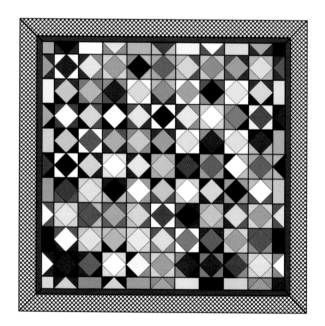

Finishing the Quilt

1. Press the quilt top carefully and mark it for quilting.

2. Layer the quilt top with the backing and batting. Baste with thread for hand quilting or with safety pins for machine quilting.

3. Quilt as desired and bind with the 2¼"-wide binding strips.

Tessellation

Materials

Yardages are based on 42"-wide fabrics.

85 strips, 2" x 42", of assorted fabrics

2¼ yards of light blue print for outer border

⅞ yard of light blue polka-dot fabric for
    inner-border blocks

4¼ yards of fabric for backing

⅝ yard of fabric for binding

76" x 76" piece of batting

Cutting

*All measurements include a ¼"-wide seam
allowance.*

From *each* of the 85 assorted fabric strips, cut:

4 rectangles, 2" x 5" (340 total)

4 rectangles, 2" x 3½" (340 total)

From the light blue polka-dot fabric, cut:

13 strips, 2" x 42"; cut into 52 rectangles,
    2" x 5", and 52 rectangles, 2" x 3½"

From the light blue print, cut on the *lengthwise* grain:

4 strips, 4½" x 76"

From the binding fabric, cut:

8 strips, 2¼" x 42"

Organizing Hint

Place each 2" x 3½" rectangle on top of a matching 2" x 5" rectangle and place them in a large box such as a pizza box. It will make it easier to select fabrics as you need them.

This is a great quilt to build from your stash. You can use
a wide variety of fabrics: Liberty, William Morris, '30s
reproductions, brights, earth tones, or a mixture of scraps.
They all work. You only need one strip from each fabric,
so it won't make a dent in your collection.

Making the Pinwheel Blocks

1. To make the first Pinwheel block, select a main fabric (you will use the whole stack) and select four different corner fabrics. For the four corners you will need only one piece of each size. Set the rest of the corner pieces aside. You will use all of them later.

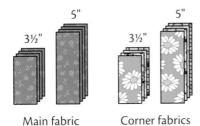

Main fabric   Corner fabrics

2. Sew the eight 2" x 3½" rectangles together on the diagonal, pairing the main fabric with each corner fabric. Press toward the main fabric.

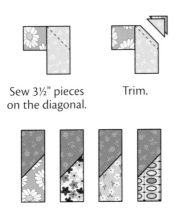

Sew 3½" pieces   Trim.
on the diagonal.

3. With the main fabric on top and right sides together, sew the four 2" x 5" main fabric rectangles along the right side of the diagonal pairs. Press.

4. Sew four 2" x 5" corner pieces to the left side of each unit from step 3, matching corner colors.

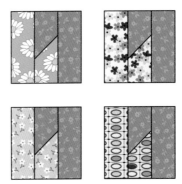

5. Sew the four sections together with the main fabric creating a pinwheel shape.

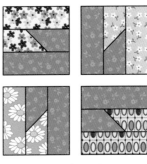

Turn the units
to make a pinwheel.

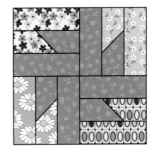

Finished block

6. For the next Pinwheel block, choose a different main fabric (pinwheel color). Match two corners (one of each size) with the previous block and select two new corners. Remember to set the remaining corners aside. Don't put them back with the full sets.

7. Work across the row until you have a row of five blocks. You can sew the pinwheels together as you complete each block.

8. For the second row, choose a new main fabric and match the two corners from above; also select two new corners.

9. For the next block, choose a new main fabric, match three adjacent corners, and select one new corner. Complete the row and sew it to the first row.

10. Complete three more rows and sew to the rows above.

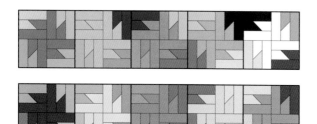

Making the Border Pinwheel Blocks

1. For the top border, select a new main fabric and match the two inside corners to the first row of the quilt. Use the blue polka-dot fabric for the two outside corners.

2. Continue to make the top border row and then the bottom. Make the side borders, continuing around the quilt until the 20 border blocks for the sides are completed and ready to sew to the quilt.

3. Make each of the four corner blocks with a new main fabric. Match one inside corner to

the quilt and use the blue polka-dot fabric for the other three corners.

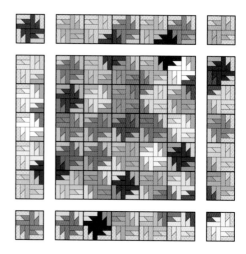

Adding the Mitered Border

Refer to "Mitered Borders" (page 8) to add the four 4½" x 76" light blue outer-border strips.

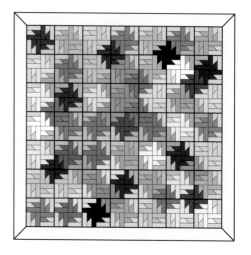

Finishing the Quilt

1. Press the quilt top carefully and mark it for quilting.

2. Layer the quilt top with the backing and batting. Baste with thread for hand quilting or with safety pins for machine quilting.

3. Quilt as desired and bind with the 2¼"-wide binding strips.

♥ Winter ♥

In the winter, I could invite friends and family to
come to eat a fabulous turkey dinner. We could play
board games or have a Ping-Pong tournament.
Or, I could bake dozens of cookies and have
an exchange with my friends. I could shop
for Valentine's Day presents for everybody.
No, I think I'd rather make a quilt, and
that would be a perfect day.

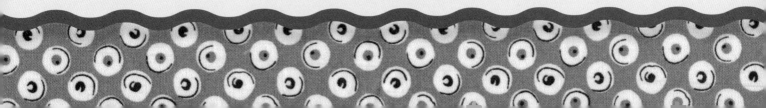

Folk-Art Christmas

Materials

Yardages are based on 42"-wide fabrics.

20 fat eighths of assorted prints for all appliqué shapes, Pineapple block backgrounds, and sashing strips

1½ yards of light green checked fabric for Tree and Ornaments block backgrounds

1 yard of medium green striped fabric for Hearts block and House block backgrounds

1 yard of yellow print for outside border (**or** 2 yards if using a directional border print)

¾ yard of light print for Holly block backgrounds

½ yard of blue checked fabric for sashing

½ yard of red print for Holly block borders

½ yard of green solid for tree and holly leaves

½ yard of blue print for House block and Hearts block borders

⅓ yard of green fabric for Ornaments block border

¼ yard of green print for Tree block border

1 fat quarter of yellow print for house

Scraps of green fabrics for holly leaves

4 yards of fabric for backing

⅝ yard of fabric for binding

67" x 69" piece of batting

3½ yards of fusible web

½ yard of interfacing

Cutting

All measurements include a ¼"-wide seam allowance. Note that all the background pieces are cut slightly oversized. They will be trimmed to the size shown AFTER the appliqué is done.

From the light print for Holly block backgrounds, cut on the *lengthwise* grain:

1 rectangle, 7½" x 22½" (will be trimmed to 6½" x 21½"; Holly block A)

1 rectangle, 7½" x 19½" (will be trimmed to 6½" x 18½"; Holly block B)

1 rectangle, 9½" x 17" (will be trimmed to 8½" x 16"; Holly block C)

From the red print, cut:

2 strips, 2" x 21½"

2 strips, 2" x 9½"

2 strips, 2½" x 18½"

2 strips, 2½" x 10½"

2 strips, 1¾" x 16"

2 strips, 1¾" x 11"

From the assorted print fat eighths, cut:

3 rectangles, 8½" x 10½" (will be trimmed to 7½" x 9½"; Pineapple blocks)

From *1* yellow fat eighth, cut:

4 sashing strips, 2½" x 9½"

*Welcome friends and family home for the holidays
with this festive Christmas quilt. You'll have fun
selecting just the right fabrics for the appliqués,
and the quilt will be a fabulous addition to
your collection of holiday decorations.*

From the medium green striped fabric, cut:

1 rectangle, 10½" x 30½" (will be trimmed to 9½" x 29½"; Hearts block)

1 square, 20½" x 20½" (will be trimmed to 19½" x 19½"; House block)

From the blue print for House block and Hearts block borders, cut:

1 strip, 2" x 42"; cut into 2 strips, 2" x 19½"

2 strips, 2" x 42"; cut into 2 strips, 2" x 22½", and 2 strips, 2" x 12½"

2 strips, 2" x 29½"

From the light green checked fabric, cut on the *lengthwise* grain:

1 rectangle, 17" x 20½" (will be trimmed to 16" x 19½"; Tree block)

1 rectangle, 10½" x 51½" (will be trimmed to 9½" x 50½"; Ornaments block)

From the green print for Tree block border, cut:

2 strips, 1¾" x 19½"

2 strips, 1¾" x 18½"

From the green fabric for Ornaments block border, cut:

4 strips, 2" x 42"

From the blue checked fabric, cut:

1 strip, 1½" x 32½"

9 strips, 1½" x 42"

From the yellow print for outside border, cut:

7 *crosswise* strips, 4" x 42"; **or** 4 *lengthwise* strips, 4" x 72"

From the binding fabric, cut:

7 strips, 2¼" x 42"

Making the Appliqué Blocks

The appliqué patterns (pages 57–60) are for the fusible-web method and do not include seam allowances. The ornaments are made with interfacing, and adding a seam allowance to the pattern is not necessary. Follow the manufacturer's instructions for the fusible web you are using and refer to "Fusible Appliqué" (page 7) to prepare the pieces. Refer to the photograph (page 51) as a guide for placing the pieces on the backgrounds.

Holly Blocks

1. Use the three light background rectangles for the Holly blocks: 7½" x 22½", 7½" x 19½", and 9½" x 17".

2. Prepare the holly leaves and berries using the patterns (page 57). Trace, fuse, cut, and iron in place using the diagrams below and the photo (page 51) for placement guidance.

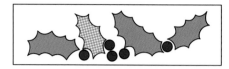

Holly block A

Holly block B

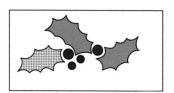

Holly block C

3. Trim Holly block A to 6½" x 21½"; trim block B to 6½" x 18½"; and trim block C to 8½" x 16".

4. Sew the red print borders around each Holly block: add the 2" red print strips to block A,

add the 2½" strips to block B, and add the 1¾" strips to block C. Press the seam allowances toward the block borders.

Pineapple Blocks

1. For the two oval pineapples, use the patterns (page 58) and fuse the shapes to the 8½" x 10½" background pieces. Stitch the edges by machine and trim the blocks to 7½" x 9½".

2. For the geometric pineapple, fuse a 2½" x 9" piece of fusible web to the wrong side of the fabric that you chose for the pineapple. Peel off the paper backing and rotary cut the fused fabric into two strips, ⅞" x 9" each.

3. Cut the strips into a total of 26 equilateral triangles using the 60° line on your ruler. Save the end triangles. Two equilateral triangles will be extra.

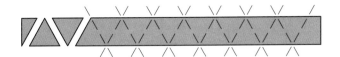

4. Arrange, fuse, and stitch the triangles onto the background fabric. Add the leaves at the bottom. Trim the block to 7½" x 9½".

5. Sew the four 2½" x 9½" sashing strips and three Pineapple blocks together as shown.

Hearts Block

1. Trace, fuse, and cut out three sets of three hearts using the patterns (page 59). Fold the 10½" x 30½" medium green background piece in half vertically to find the center. Arrange the hearts on the background piece, fuse, and stitch. Trim the block to 9½" x 29½".

Crease

2. Sew the 2" x 29½" blue print border strips to the sides and press toward the border strips. Sew the 2" x 12½" blue print border strips to the top and bottom. Press.

Tree Block

1. Make a template for the tree using the pattern (pages 59 and 60).

2. Fold a 14" x 19" piece of fusible web in half lengthwise. Place the tree template on the folded line. Trace the tree. Flip the tree template over and trace the tree on other half of the fusible web.

3. Iron the rectangle of fusible web to the wrong side of the green fabric.

4. Cut out the tree, peel off the paper, and center it on the 17" x 20½" light green checked background piece. Fuse in place.

5. Trace, fuse, and cut circle ornaments using the patterns (page 60). Fuse them to the background piece using the photograph as a guide. Stitch around all the appliqué pieces. Trim the block to 16" x 19½".

6. Sew the 1¾" x 19½" green print strips to the sides and press. Sew the 1¾" x 18½" green print strips to the top and bottom; press.

House Block

1. Iron an 11" x 13" piece of fusible web to the wrong side of the yellow print fabric for the house. Rotary cut a 10" x 12" rectangle.

2. Iron fusible web to the other fabrics for the house and use the dimensions given below to cut the remaining pieces.

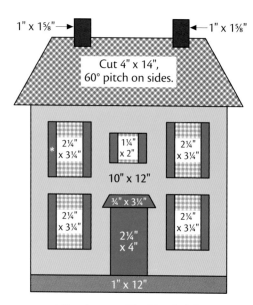

1" x 1⅝" →   ← 1" x 1⅝"

Cut 4" x 14", 60° pitch on sides.

2¼" x 3¼"   1¼" x 2"   2¼" x 3¼"

10" x 12"

¾" x 3¼"

2¼" x 3¼"   2¼" x 3¼"

2¼" x 4"

1" x 12"

* Cut shutters ¾" wide x height of respective window.

3. Fuse the pieces onto the 20½" x 20½" medium green background piece.

4. Stitch around all the pieces and trim the block to 19½" x 19½".

5. Sew the 2" x 19½" blue print strips to the sides and press toward the borders. Add the 2" x 22½" strips to the top and bottom; press.

Ornaments Block

The ornaments are appliquéd using the fusible interfacing method, which makes for perfectly smooth appliquéd circles. Refer to "Interfacing Appliqué" (page 7) for additional details.

1. Use a CD or the pattern (page 57) to make a template and trace it eight times onto the smooth side of the fusible interfacing. Allow for a ¼" seam around each circle.

2. Sew interfacing circles onto the right side of your chosen fabrics. Cut out ¼" away from stitching line.

3. Make a small slit in the interfacing and turn right side out. Use a blunt tool to smooth out the seam.

4. Arrange the ornaments on the 10½" x 51½" light green checked background. When you are happy with the placement, iron in place.

5. Add the hook caps with fusible web and embroider a loop if you wish.

6. Stitch around the ornaments and then trim the block to 9½" x 50½".

7. Piece together the four 2" x 42" green strips and cut into two strips, 2" x 50½", and two strips, 2" x 12½". Sew the 2" x 50½" green strips to the top and bottom and press. Sew the 2" x 12½" strips to the sides and press.

Assembling the Quilt

1. Sew Holly block A to the left of the Pineapple block.

2. Piece together the nine 1½" x 42" blue checked sashing strips and trim to four strips, 1½" x 53½", and two strips, 1½" x 57½". Sew 1½" x 53½" strips to the top and bottom of the Holly and Pineapple blocks unit.

3. Sew the Tree block to the top of Holly block C. Then sew the Hearts block to the Tree and Holly blocks unit.

4. Sew the House block to the bottom of Holly block B.

5. Sew the 1½" x 32½" blue checked sashing strip to the right of the Hearts, Tree, and Holly blocks section.

6. Sew the House and Holly blocks unit to the right side of the unit from step 5.

7. Sew the Holly and Pineapple blocks section to the top of the quilt.

8. Add a 1½" x 53½" blue checked sashing strip to the bottom of the quilt.

9. Sew the Ornaments block to the bottom of the quilt.

10. Add a 1½" x 53½" blue checked sashing strip to bottom of the Ornaments block.

11. Sew the two 1½" x 57½" blue checked sashing strips to the sides of the quilt.

Making the Mitered Border

Refer to "Mitered Borders" (page 8) and add the four 4" x 72" border strips to the quilt (piece seven 42" strips together and cut to the needed length if you cut the border fabric crosswise).

Finishing the Quilt

1. Press the quilt top carefully and mark it for quilting.

2. Layer the quilt top with the backing and batting. Baste with thread for hand quilting or with safety pins for machine quilting.

3. Quilt as desired and bind with the 2¼"-wide binding strips.

Quilting Suggestion

Use the diagram below to help you quilt around the geometric pineapple in one continuous line.

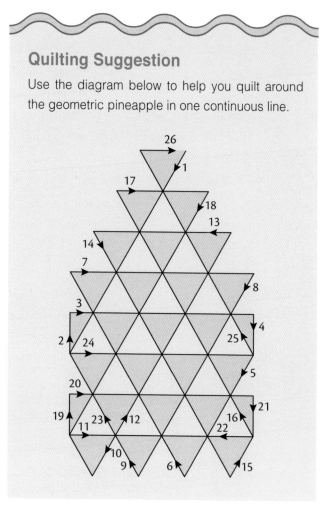

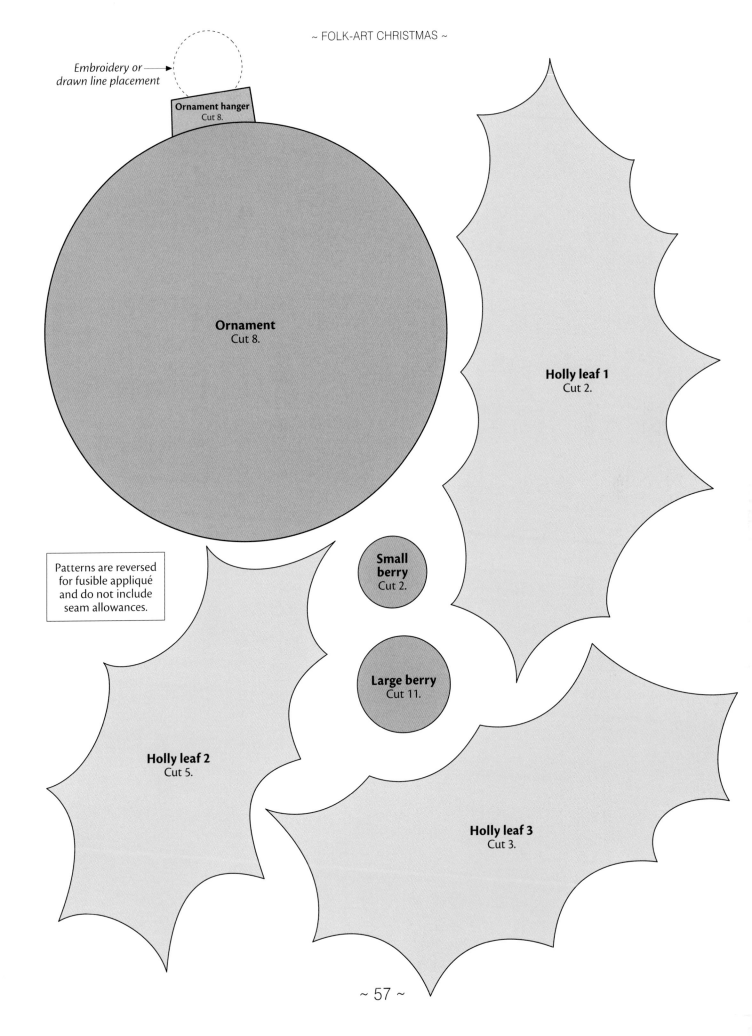

Embroidery or drawn line placement

Ornament hanger
Cut 8.

Ornament
Cut 8.

Holly leaf 1
Cut 2.

Patterns are reversed for fusible appliqué and do not include seam allowances.

Small berry
Cut 2.

Large berry
Cut 11.

Holly leaf 2
Cut 5.

Holly leaf 3
Cut 3.

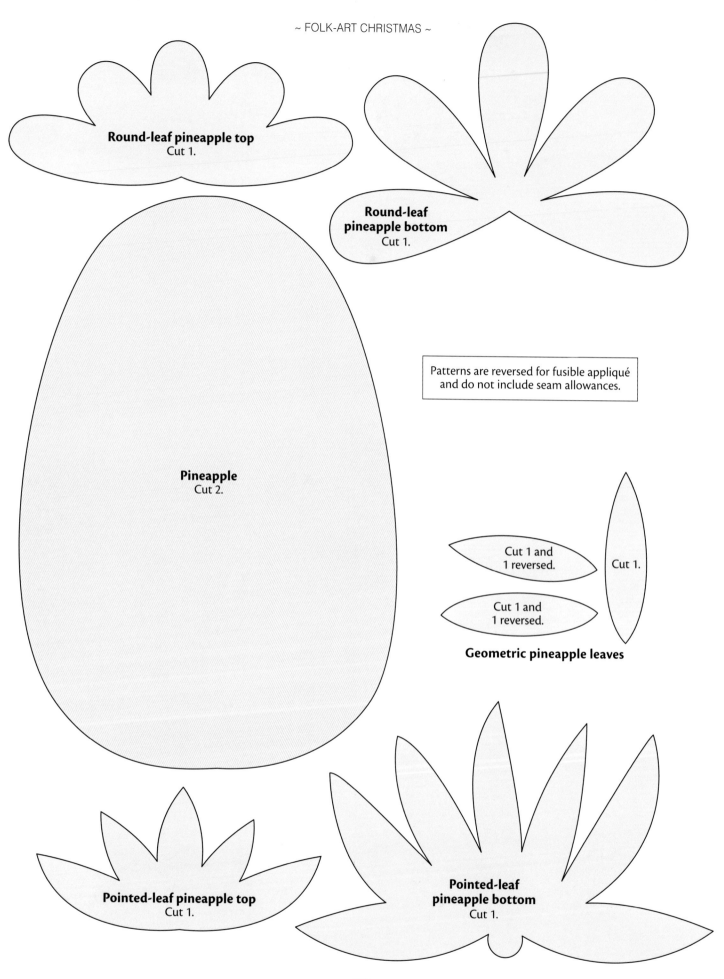

Round-leaf pineapple top
Cut 1.

**Round-leaf
pineapple bottom**
Cut 1.

Patterns are reversed for fusible appliqué
and do not include seam allowances.

Pineapple
Cut 2.

Cut 1 and
1 reversed.

Cut 1.

Cut 1 and
1 reversed.

Geometric pineapple leaves

Pointed-leaf pineapple top
Cut 1.

**Pointed-leaf
pineapple bottom**
Cut 1.

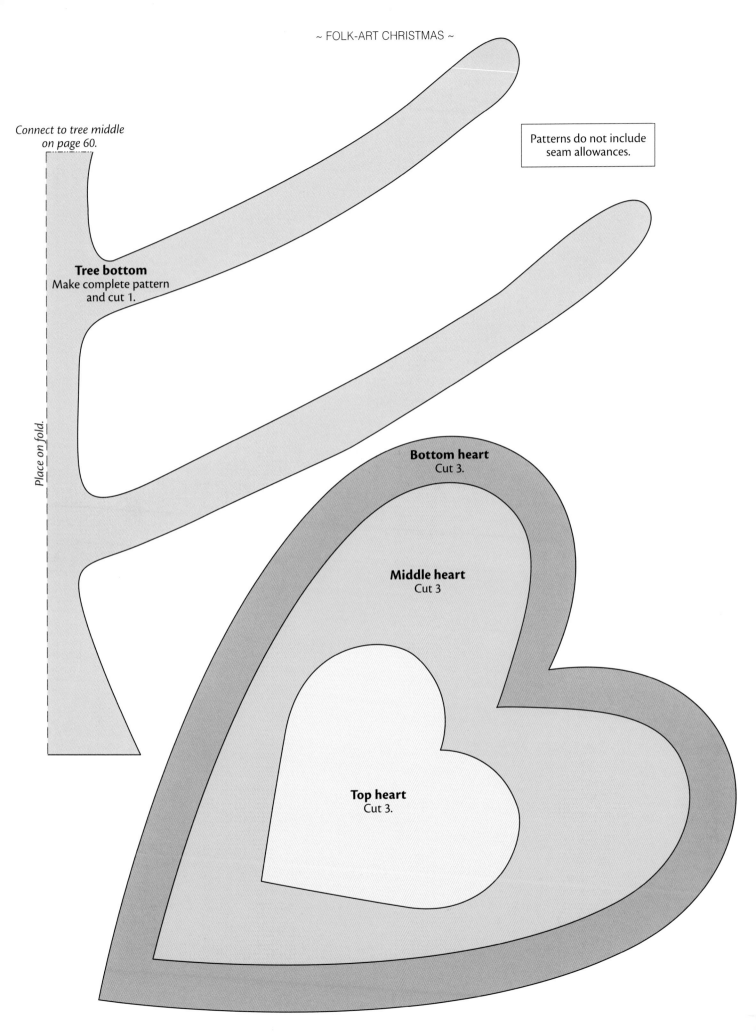

Connect to tree middle on page 60.

Patterns do not include seam allowances.

Place on fold.

Tree bottom
Make complete pattern and cut 1.

Bottom heart
Cut 3.

Middle heart
Cut 3

Top heart
Cut 3.

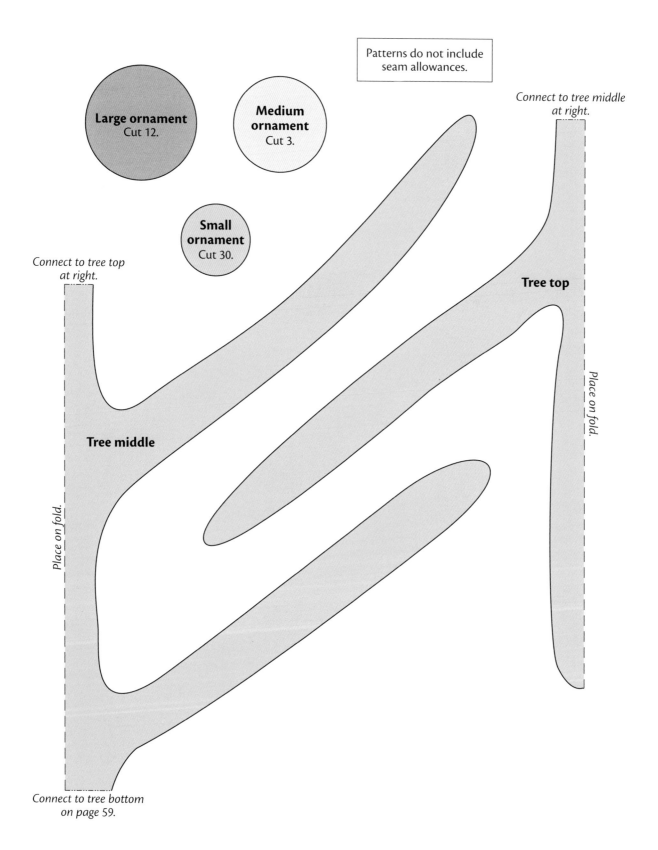

Patterns do not include
seam allowances.

Large ornament
Cut 12.

Medium
ornament
Cut 3.

Small
ornament
Cut 30.

Connect to tree middle
at right.

Tree top

Place on fold.

Connect to tree top
at right.

Tree middle

Place on fold.

Connect to tree bottom
on page 59.

Snowy Peaks

Materials

Yardages are based on 42"-wide fabrics.

3¾ yards of unbleached muslin

1¾ yards *total* of blue prints

1½ yards *total* of pink and red prints

1½ yards *total* of green prints

1¼ yards *total* of yellow and gold prints

¾ yard *total* of orange and peach prints

½ yard *total* of black prints

4½ yards of fabric for backing

⅝ yard of fabric for binding*

79" x 77" piece of batting

Equilateral-triangle ruler**

You can also cut strips from leftover fabrics and make a scrappy pieced binding as I did on my quilt.

**If you don't have one of these, they're available at www.AmericanJane.com.*

Cutting

All measurements include a ¼"-wide seam allowance.

From the unbleached muslin, cut:

59 strips, 2½" x 42"

From the assorted prints, cut a *total* of:

59 strips, 2½" x 42"

From the binding fabric, cut:

8 strips, 2¼" x 42"

Making the Diamonds

1. Layer each muslin strip with a print strip, right sides together. Sew both long sides with a ¼" seam until you have 57 pairs sewn. Leave the remaining two pairs unsewn.

2. Align the 2½" line on an equilateral-triangle ruler with the bottom raw edge of the sewn strips. Cut on both sides.

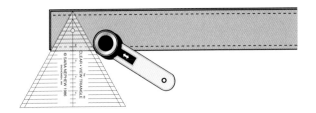

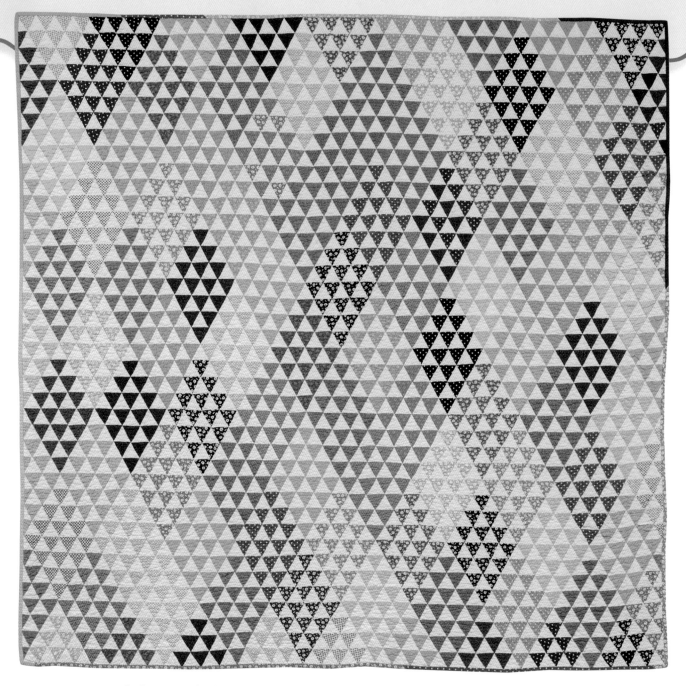

*Crisp and clear as a snow-capped mountain on a winter
day, these diamonds are a girl's best friend. A simple
strip-piecing technique makes quick work of the pieced
diamonds—this technique is sure to become
a quilter's best friend as well.*

3. Move the ruler over to the right, keeping the 2½" line on the bottom raw edge and the lower-left side at the point of your previous cut. Repeat to the end of the strip and for all remaining pairs of strips, including the unsewn strips. Set the cut triangles from the unsewn strips aside until later.

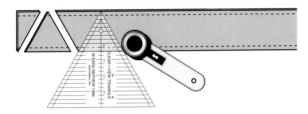

4. Use a seam ripper to open the tips of the sewn triangles to create a diamond. Press the seam allowances toward the print triangles.

Making the Large Diamond Blocks

To make one Large Diamond block, sew 16 small diamonds of the same color into pairs, keeping the light triangles toward the top. Sew the pairs into four diagonal rows. Sew the rows together in pairs. Match the "bunny ear" seam points to help align the diamonds. Press toward the prints. Sew the rows together to complete the block. Construct a total of 76 Large Diamond blocks.

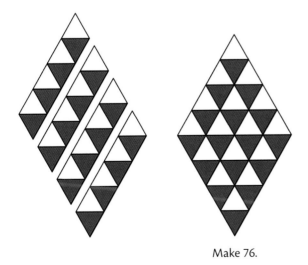

Make 76.

Making Half Blocks for the Sides

You will need five half blocks for the left side and five half blocks for the right side of the quilt.

1. For each half block, sew a row of four diamonds, a row of three diamonds, and a row of two diamonds as shown, matching the colors.

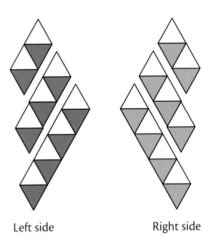

Left side   Right side

2. Sew the rows together and add a single diamond to the top corner of the 10 half blocks as shown. You will trim off the long edge of the half Diamond blocks after final assembly.

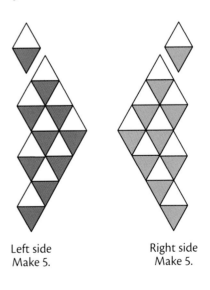

Left side   Right side
Make 5.   Make 5.

Making Half Blocks for the Top and Bottom

You'll need nine half blocks for the top and nine half blocks for the bottom of the quilt.

1. For each of the top half blocks, sew together a row of three diamonds and a row of two diamonds, starting from the right and matching the colors. Add a single diamond, and then add a single print triangle (set aside earlier) to the top of each row and one additional triangle to the upper-left corner. Sew the rows together to complete a top half block. Repeat to make nine.

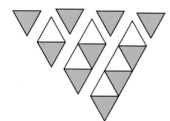 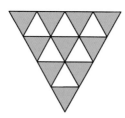

Top half Diamond block.
Make 9.

2. For each of the bottom half blocks, sew together a row of three diamonds and a row of two diamonds, starting from the left and matching the colors. Add a single diamond, and then add a single muslin triangle to the bottom of each row and one additional muslin triangle to the lower-right corner. Sew the rows together to complete a bottom half block. Repeat to make nine.

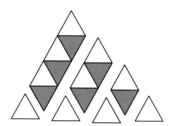 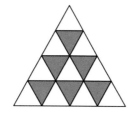

Bottom half Diamond block.
Make 9.

Assembling the Blocks

1. Arrange the blocks on a design wall or a large piece of flannel. Sew the blocks into diagonal rows; then sew the rows together.

2. Trim the left and right side half blocks to make straight side edges.

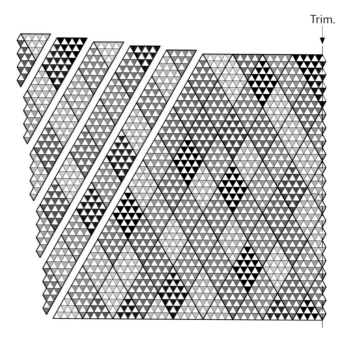

Trim.

Finishing the Quilt

1. Press the quilt top carefully and mark it for quilting.

2. Layer the quilt top with the backing and batting. Baste with thread for hand quilting or with safety pins for machine quilting.

3. Quilt as desired and bind with the 2¼"-wide binding strips.

Be Mine

Materials

Yardages are based on 42"-wide fabrics.

3 yards *total* of assorted large- and small-scale red, blue, green, and yellow floral prints for hearts

2¾ yards *total* of assorted red-on-white prints for appliqué backgrounds

11 fat eighths *total* of medium-value checked fabric and polka-dot fabric for smallest heart backgrounds

4 fat quarters *total* of medium-value checked fabric and polka-dot fabric for center heart appliqué backgrounds

¾ yard *total* of assorted light floral prints for smallest hearts

⅜ yard of red polka-dot fabric for inner border*

4 yards of fabric for backing

⅝ yard of fabric for binding

69" x 69" piece of batting

4 yards of lightweight fusible interfacing **or** fusible web

*If you want to fussy cut a polka-dot fabric as I did, purchase extra yardage.

Cutting

All measurements include a ¼"-wide seam allowance.

From *each* fat quarter of medium-value checked fabric and polka-dot fabric, cut:

1 square, 12½" x 12½" (4 total)

From the fat eighths of medium-value checked fabric and polka-dot fabric, cut a *total* of:

44 squares, 4½" x 4½"

From the assorted red-on-white prints, cut:

20 squares, 6½" x 6½"

28 squares, 8½" x 8½"

From the red polka-dot fabric, cut:

2 strips, 2½" x 36½"

2 strips, 2½" x 40½"

From the binding fabric, cut:

7 strips, 2¼" x 42"

This bright quilt was inspired by those little candy hearts
with short sayings on them. With this quilt you can truly
say to that special someone, "I love you with all
my hearts"—all 96 of them.

Making the Appliqué Blocks

The instructions are written for using fusible interfacing. For details, see "Interfacing Appliqué" (page 7). If you want to use fusible web, refer to "Fusible Appliqué" (page 7).

1. Trace all the heart patterns onto the smooth side of lightweight interfacing. Allow a ¼" seam allowance beyond your traced line. The traced line will be your sewing line.

2. Place the interfacing on the heart fabric with the bumpy side facing the right side of the fabric. Sew the 12", 8", and 6" hearts to the assorted floral prints. Sew the 4" hearts to the light floral prints.

3. Cut out each heart, leaving a ¼" seam allowance. Cut a small slit in the interfacing and clip the V of the heart. Turn the hearts right side out. Use a small pressing tool, chopstick, or pen to push the seam out and smooth the edges.

4. Iron a 12" heart to a 12½" background square and stitch around it with a machine-appliqué stitch. Make a total of four 12" hearts.

5. Repeat the process to appliqué hearts on the diagonal onto four of *each* of the 8½", 6½", and 4½" background squares. These will be used in the corners. Appliqué a total of twenty-eight 8" hearts on the 8½" background squares, twenty 6" hearts on the 6½" background squares, and forty-four 4" hearts on the 4½" background squares.

Assembling the Quilt Top

1. Sew the four 12½" blocks together to make the center of the quilt. I made each heart point in a different direction.

2. Sew four sets of four 6½" hearts together. Sew two sets to opposite sides of large-heart unit.

3. Add the corner diagonal hearts to the remaining two sets and sew the sets to the top and bottom of the unit.

4. For the inner border, sew the two red polka-dot 2½" x 36½" strips to the sides of the quilt. Then add the two 2½" x 40½" strips to the top and bottom.

5. Sew four sets of ten 4½" hearts together.

6. Sew two sets to opposite sides of the quilt.

7. Add the corner diagonal hearts to the remaining two sets and sew the sets to the top and bottom of the quilt.

8. Sew four sets of six 8½" hearts together.

9. Sew two sets to opposite sides of the quilt. Add the corner diagonal hearts to the remaining two sets and sew the sets to the top and bottom of the quilt.

Finishing the Quilt

1. Press the quilt top carefully and mark it for quilting.

2. Layer the quilt top with the backing and batting. Baste with thread for hand quilting or with safety pins for machine quilting.

3. Quilt as desired and bind with the 2¼"-wide binding strips.

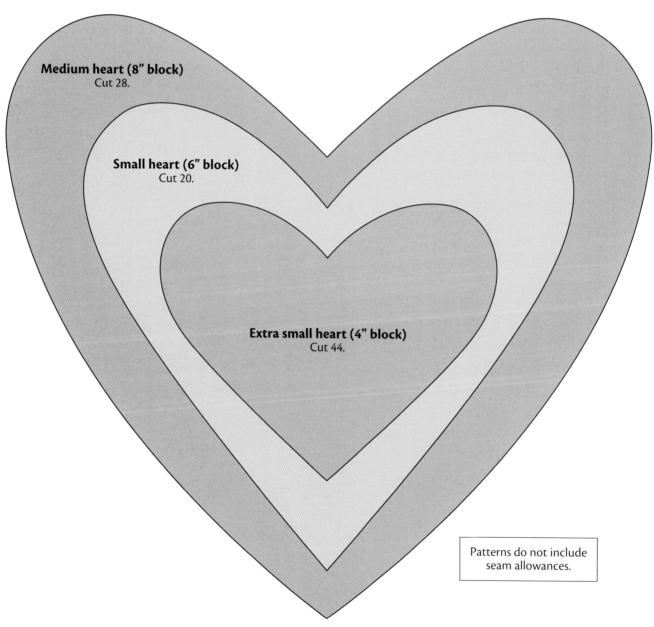

Medium heart (8" block)
Cut 28.

Small heart (6" block)
Cut 20.

Extra small heart (4" block)
Cut 44.

Patterns do not include seam allowances.

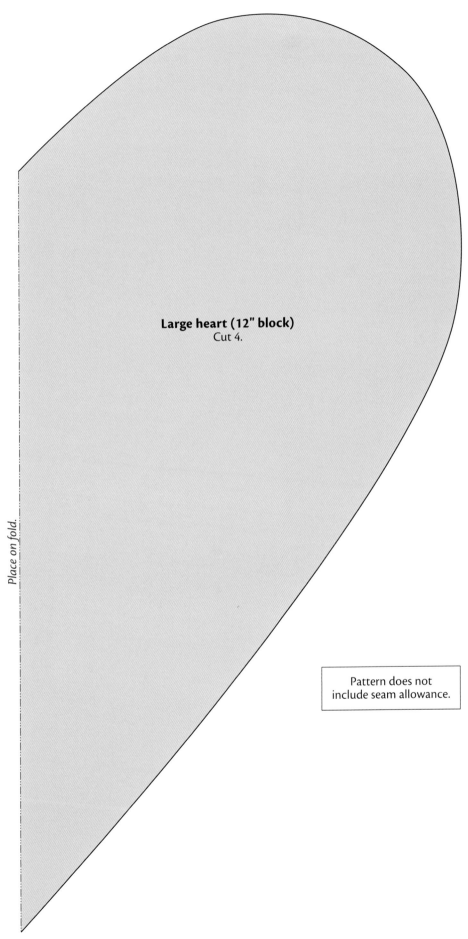

Large heart (12" block)
Cut 4.

Place on fold.

Pattern does not include seam allowance.

All Stars

Choosing Fabrics

Choosing fabrics for a scrappy quilt like this one is easier than choosing just two or three fabrics. When you use only a few fabrics, each one plays a very important role to create a balanced quilt with interest. For this quilt, you will need 54 fabrics for the stars unless you repeat some fabrics. Select your color scheme, and then choose nine fabrics at a time. This is a good time to dip into your stash because you need only one to five 1½" strips of any particular fabric.

In my quilt, the first border is cut from a printed border fabric. For border-print fabrics, it is wise to buy the length needed so that you don't have to piece it. The second border is cut crosswise and pieced.

Materials

Yardages are based on 42"-wide fabrics. Note that in this list, the word medium *refers to value.*

4⅝ yards of light print for background

2⅝ yards of border print for inner border*

⅞ yard of medium print for outer border

⅛ yard *each* of 6 dark prints for Star fabric 1

⅛ yard *each* of 6 medium light prints for Star fabric 2

¼ yard *each* of 6 medium dark prints for Star fabric 3

¼ yard *each* of 6 medium light prints for Star fabric 4

⅓ yard *each* of 6 medium dark prints for Star fabric 5

¼ yard *each* of 6 medium light prints for Star fabric 6

¼ yard *each* of 6 medium dark prints for Star fabric 7

⅛ yard *each* of 6 medium light prints for Star fabric 8

⅛ yard *each* of 6 dark prints for Star fabric 9

7¾ yards of fabric for backing

¾ yard of fabric for binding

93" x 99" piece of batting

Plastic template material

This yardage is based on lengthwise cutting from a border print. If you cut crosswise and piece strips together, ¾ yard will be enough.

This quilt is easier to make than it looks. Strip piecing and angled cutting make quick work of all those little diamonds. There are set-in seams, but if you follow the Y-seams rule on page 7, you will have no problem. This is the perfect quilt for a winter's project.

Cutting

All measurements include a ¼"-wide seam allowance.

From the Star fabrics, cut:

1 strip, 1½" x 42", of *each* fabric 1 (6 total)

2 strips, 1½" x 42", of *each* fabric 2 (12 total)

3 strips, 1½" x 42", of *each* fabric 3 (18 total)

4 strips, 1½" x 42", of *each* fabric 4 (24 total)

5 strips, 1½" x 42", of *each* fabric 5 (30 total)

4 strips, 1½" x 42", of *each* fabric 6 (24 total)

3 strips, 1½" x 42", of *each* fabric 7 (18 total)

2 strips, 1½" x 42", of *each* fabric 8 (12 total)

1 strip, 1½" x 42", of each Star fabric 9
   (6 total)

From the light print, cut:

12 strips, 10½" x 42"

3 strips, 5½" x 42"

2 strips, 3½" x 42"

From the border print for inner border, cut:

4 strips, 2½" x 90", **or** 9 strips, 2½" x 42"

From the medium print for outer border, cut:

10 strips, 2½" x 42"

From the fabric for binding, cut:

10 strips, 2¼" x 42"

Making the Star Blocks

1. Choose the nine fabrics (select one from each group of fabrics 1 through 9) that you want for one Star block.

2. Sew 1½" x 42" strips cut from Star fabrics 1–9 into five sets of five strips each as shown. Press in the direction shown by the arrows.

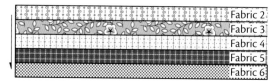

Strip set for row 1

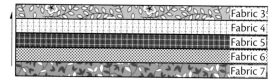

Strip set for row 2

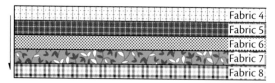

Strip set for row 3

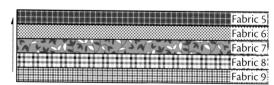

Strip set for row 4

Strip set for row 5

3. Place the first strip set on a cutting mat. Cut off a corner at a 60° angle. Refer to "Angled Cuts" (page 6) if you are not familiar with using the angle lines on your ruler. Move the ruler over and cut six segments at 1½" intervals. Each segment will be a row 1. Set aside the remainder of the strip set. Repeat for the remaining strip sets to cut rows 2–5.

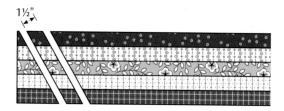

4. Sew rows 1 and 2 together, offsetting the strips by ¼" at each end. Add rows 3, 4, and 5 to form a diamond. Press all the seam allowances away from the center (row 1). Repeat to make six diamonds.

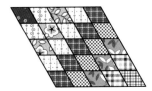

Diamond assembly

5. Sew the six diamonds together to form a Star block. Begin and end your stitching ¼" from where the seams will intersect at the edges, following "The Rule of Y Seams" (page 7). Do not sew into the seam allowance.

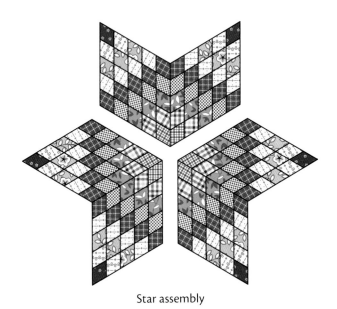

Star assembly

6. Using the remainder of the strip sets, cut 12 additional segments to make two more blocks. Repeat steps 4 and 5.

Star Assembly

From each strip set you can make three Star blocks and one half block. You will need 18 Star blocks and four half blocks. Change the orientation of the pieced diamond units so that the outer points are in the center when assembling some of the Star blocks made from the same strip sets; this will add variety.

7. Follow steps 1–6 for five more strip sets. Make a total of 18 blocks.

8. Use the remainder of the strip sets to make four half blocks, cutting three 1½" segments for each.

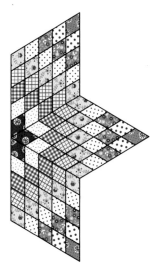

Make 4.

Adding the Background Hexagons

1. Make templates for the hexagon, half hexagon, and triangle using the patterns (pages 75 and 76).

2. Cut 34 hexagons from the 10½" x 42" strips of background fabric. You can layer strips of fabric to cut more than one at a time.

3. Cut 12 half hexagons from the 5½" x 42" strips.

4. Cut eight triangles from the 3½" x 42" strips.

Setting In the Background Hexagons

There is no set rule for sewing in the background hexagons, but I find it easier to sew them in rows. No matter what, there are a lot of short set-in or Y seams; just remember to begin and end ¼" from the edge of each seam. Take your time, and your quilt will come together perfectly.

5. For the top and bottom rows, use three full hexagons, two half hexagons, and four triangles each. Trim off the excess along the top and bottom, leaving a ¼" seam allowance beyond all star points.

Mitering the Borders

1. Piece the ten 2½" x 42" strips together for the outer border to make four 2½" x 98" border strips.

2. Piece the inner-border strips if you are using 42" strips; make four 2½" x 90" strips. Sew the inner-border and outer-border strips together in pairs to make four border units, centering the shorter inner border on the longer outer border. Press the seam allowances toward the outer border.

3. Referring to "Mitered Borders" (page 8), add the borders to the quilt.

Finishing the Quilt

1. Press the quilt top carefully and mark it for quilting.

2. Layer the quilt top with the backing and batting. Baste with thread for hand quilting or with safety pins for machine quilting.

3. Quilt as desired and bind with the 2¼"-wide binding strips.

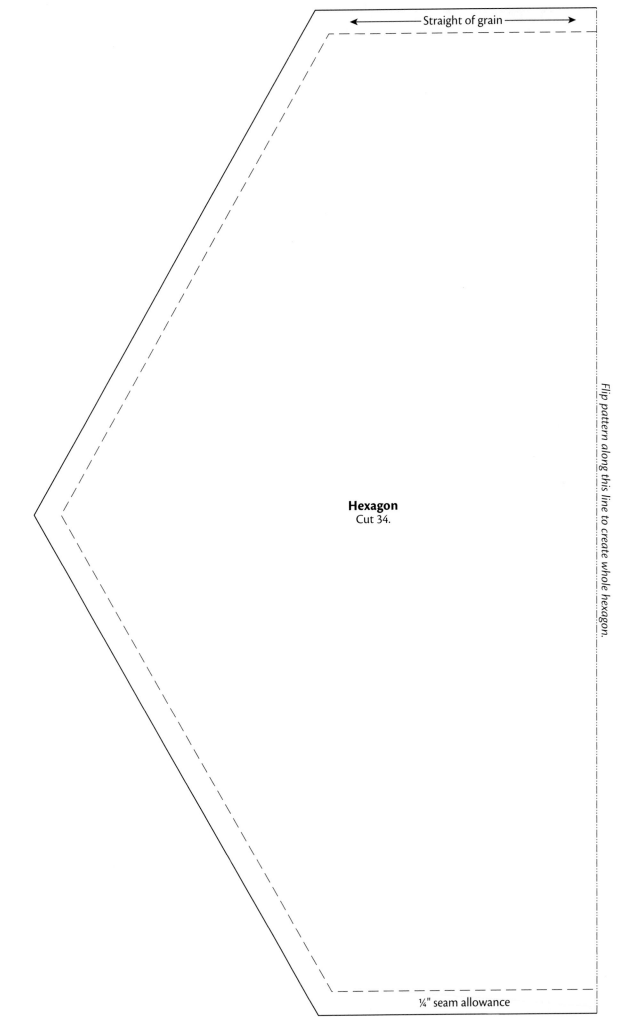

Straight of grain

Hexagon
Cut 34.

Flip pattern along this line to create whole hexagon.

¼" seam allowance

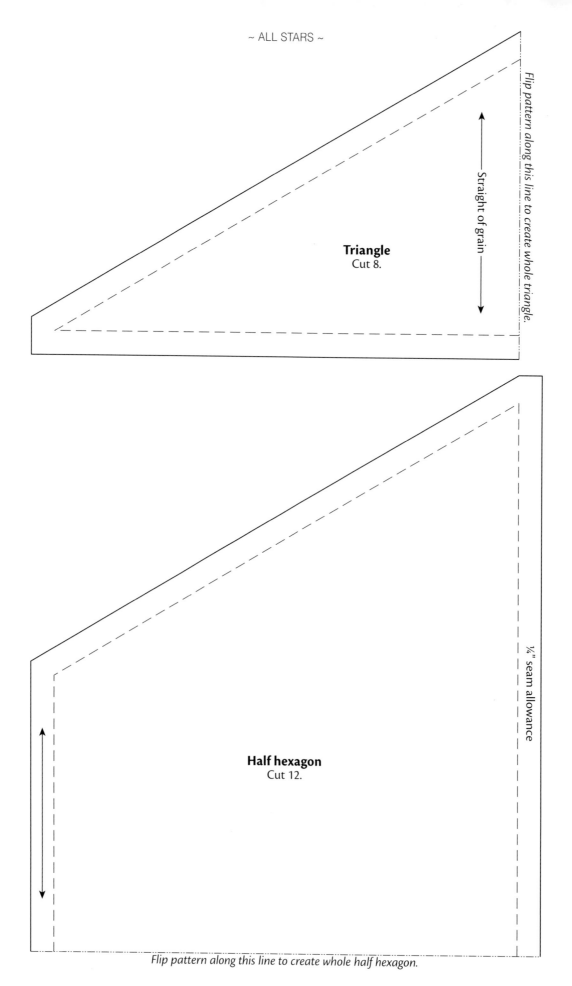

Triangle
Cut 8.

Straight of grain

Flip pattern along this line to create whole triangle.

Half hexagon
Cut 12.

¼" seam allowance

Flip pattern along this line to create whole half hexagon.

Spring

On a day in spring, I could clean the house from top to bottom. I could wash all the windows and shake out the rugs. Or, I could dig a new garden, build a fence around it, and plant daisies. However, I think I'd rather make a quilt. And that would make any day a perfect day.

Puppy Parade

Skill level: Beginner

Finished quilt: 51" x 51"

Finished pieced block: 12" x 12"

Finished appliquéd block: 10" x 12½"

Materials

Yardages are based on 42"-wide fabrics.

½ yard *each* of 4 assorted gold prints for appliqué backgrounds

1½ yards of black solid for sashing, appliqués, and narrow border

1¼ yards of gold print for center blocks, outer border, and binding

⅝ yard of red print for center blocks

⅓ yard of black print for inner border

⅛ yard of gray print for collars

12 pieces, 5" x 7" *each*, of assorted red plaids for coats

3 yards of fabric for backing

55" x 55" piece of batting

2 yards of fusible web

Cutting

All measurements include a ¼"-wide seam allowance.

From the assorted gold prints for appliqué backgrounds, cut:

12 rectangles, 11½" x 14"

From the red print, cut:

9 strips, 1½" x 42"

8 squares, 3½" x 3½"

From the gold print for center blocks, outer border, and binding, cut:

9 strips, 1½" x 42"

8 squares, 3½" x 3½"

5 strips, 1½" x 42"

6 binding strips, 2¼" x 42"

From the black solid, cut on the *lengthwise* grain:

2 strips, 1" x 12½"

1 strip, 1" x 25"

2 strips, 1" x 48"

2 strips, 1" x 49"

From the black print, cut:

2 strips, 2" x 25"

2 strips, 2" x 28"

Puppies and babies always make us say, "Aww."
Why not make this fresh quilt for the next new baby
in your life, or make it to simply celebrate spring,
the season of new beginnings?

Making the Center Blocks

1. Sew three 1½" x 42" red strips together with three 1½" x 42" gold strips, alternating the colors to make a strip set. Press toward the red strips. Make three strip sets.

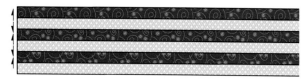

Make 3 strip sets.

2. Subcut two strip sets into 16 segments, 3½" wide, and one strip set into 24 segments, 1½" wide.

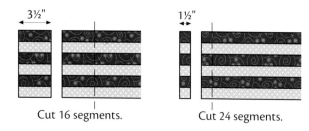

3½"

1½"

Cut 16 segments.　　　Cut 24 segments.

3. Sew six of the 1½"-wide segments into a checkerboard, rotating every other segment to make a unit of six rows of six squares. Repeat to make four.

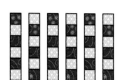

Make 4.

4. Sew a 3½" seg-ment from step 2 to each side of these units. Add 3½" red and gold squares to each corner according to the diagram.

Make 4.

5. Sew two blocks together with a 1" x 12½" black sashing strip in between. Repeat for the other two blocks.

6. Sew the block rows from step 5 together with a 1" x 25" black sashing strip in between.

7. Add the 2" x 25" black print strips to the sides of the center unit and press toward the black strips. Add the 2" x 28" black print strips to the top and bottom; press.

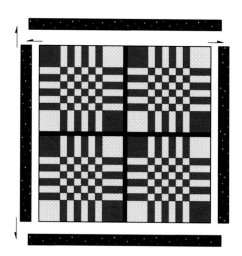

Making the Appliqué Blocks

1. Trace all pattern pieces (pages 82–83) for each fabric in a group onto the paper side of fusible web.

2. Iron the fusible web to the wrong side of the fabrics.

3. Cut out the pattern on the traced line. Remove the paper backing.

4. Referring to the diagram, arrange the pieces on the 11½" x 14" assorted gold background rectangles. Fuse in place.

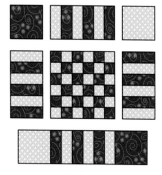

5. Stitch around each piece with an appliqué stitch using matching thread on top and a neutral thread in the bobbin.

6. Trim the background pieces to 10½" x 13".

Adding the Scottie Dog Blocks to the Quilt

1. Sew the Scottie Dog blocks together in sets of three. They will be added to the quilt top using a partial seam.

Sew in sets of 3.

2. Referring to the diagram, sew the first set of three dogs to the bottom of the center unit, but do not complete the seam on the left-hand corner. Stop 6" to 8" from the end of the quilt. Working counterclockwise, sew on the remaining sets of three dogs. Complete the first seam after the fourth group of three is sewn on.

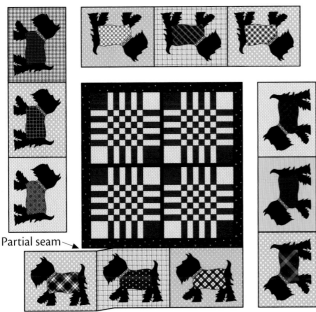

Partial seam

Work in this direction. ➞

Adding the Outer Borders

1. Sew the 1" x 48" black strips to the top and bottom and the 1" x 49" strips to the sides.

2. Using the five 1½" x 42" gold strips, piece together two borders, 1½" x 49", and two borders, 1½" x 51". Sew the shorter borders to the top and bottom and the longer ones to the sides.

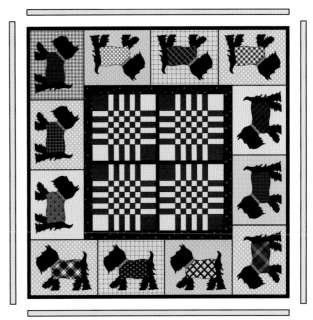

Finishing the Quilt

1. Press the quilt top carefully and mark it for quilting.

2. Layer the quilt top with the backing and batting. Baste with thread for hand quilting or with safety pins for machine quilting.

3. Quilt as desired and bind with the 2¼"-wide gold binding strips.

Patterns are reversed for fusible appliqué
and do not include seam allowances.

Collar
Cut 12.

Coat
Cut 12.

Connect to Scotty front on page 83 to complete pattern.

Scotty back
Cut 12.

Scotty front
Cut 12.

Connect to Scotty back on page 82 to complete pattern.

Daisy Dew

Skill level: Advanced

Finished quilt: 72½" x 72½"

Materials

Yardages are based on 42"-wide fabrics.

2⅛ yards of pink print for Ocean Waves center, daisy border, and outer border

1⅓ yards *total* of light prints for outer border

1 yard of red print 1 for outer border

⅞ yard of red print 2 for rickrack border

1 yard *total* of assorted prints for appliquéd leaves, stems, and flower centers

⅞ yard of yellow print 1 for rickrack border

¼ yard of yellow print 2 for appliquéd scallop border

⅛ yard *each* of 6 assorted dark prints for Ocean Waves center

⅛ yard *each* of 6 assorted light prints for Ocean Waves center

⅝ yard *total* of assorted light fabrics for appliquéd flower petals

⅓ yard of blue checked fabric for narrow border 1

⅓ yard of light print 1 for narrow border 2

⅓ yard of green print for narrow border 3

⅓ yard of light print 2 for narrow border 4

⅓ yard of red print for narrow border 5

4½ yards of fabric for backing

⅝ yard of fabric for binding

77" x 77" piece of batting

3½ yards of fusible web (optional)

½ yard of fusible interfacing

Freezer paper or heat-resistant template material

Spray starch

Cutting

All measurements include a ¼"-wide seam allowance.

From *each* of the 6 assorted dark prints, cut:

36 squares, 1⅞" x 1⅞"; cut each square once diagonally to yield 72 triangles (432 total)

From *each* of the 6 assorted light prints, cut:

36 squares, 1⅞" x 1⅞"; cut each square once diagonally to yield 72 triangles (432 total)

From the pink print, cut on the *lengthwise* grain:

1 strip, 11" x 49"; cut into 2 rectangles, 11" x 24½"

2 rectangles, 11" x 45½"

From the remainder of the pink print, cut:

2 squares, 7¼" x 7¼"; cut each square twice diagonally to yield 8 triangles

4 squares, 4¾" x 4¾"

11 strips, 2½" x 42"; cut 10 strips into 60 rectangles, 2½" x 6½"

There's something new at every turn in this medallion quilt. Surrounding the center of Ocean Waves blocks, multiple border rounds offer a change and a chance to learn a new technique or practice perfecting your piecing and appliqué skills.

From red print 2, cut:

10 strips, 2" x 42"; cut into 120 rectangles, 2" x 3¼"

1 strip, 1⅜" x 42"

From yellow print 1, cut:

12 strips, 2" x 42"; cut into 240 squares, 2" x 2"

4 squares, 2⅛" x 2⅛"; cut each square once diagonally to yield 8 triangles

4 squares, 2⅜" x 2⅜"; cut each square once diagonally to yield 8 triangles

From the blue checked fabric for narrow border 1, cut:

6 strips, 1½" x 42"

From light print 1 for narrow border 2, cut:

6 strips, 1½" x 42"

From the green print for narrow border 3, cut:

6 strips, 1¼" x 42"

From light print 2 for narrow border 4, cut:

6 strips, 1½" x 42"

From the red print for narrow border 5, cut:

6 strips, 1½" x 42"

From red print 1, cut:

11 strips, 2½" x 42"; cut 10 strips into 60 rectangles, 2½" x 6½"

From the light prints for outer border, cut:

240 squares, 2½" x 2½"

4 squares, 4⅞" x 4⅞"; cut each square once diagonally to yield 8 triangles

4 squares, 2⅞" x 2⅞"; cut each square once diagonally to yield 8 triangles

From the binding fabric, cut:

8 strips, 2¼" x 42"

Making the Ocean Waves Center

1. Using 384 light and 384 dark 1⅞" triangles, make 384 half-square-triangle units. Sew nine half-square-triangle units together to make 32 square units, 3½" x 3½", as shown.

Make 384.

Make 32.

2. Sew 20 of the units from step 1 into five blocks, rotating the direction of light and dark triangles as shown.

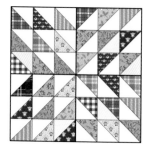

Make 4.

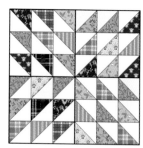

Make 1.

3. Sew two of the units from step 1 to make a rectangle as shown. Repeat to make four rectangles.

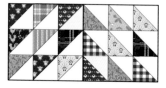

Make 4.

4. Use the remaining half-square-triangle units and light and dark triangles to make 16 triangle units with dark edges and 16 triangle units with light edges.

Make 16.

Make 16.

5. Use eight triangle units with light edges and eight triangle units with dark edges to make eight rectangles with a pink print 7¼" triangle in between as shown.

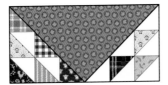

Make 8.

6. Use the 16 remaining triangle units and pink 4¾" square to make four blocks as shown.

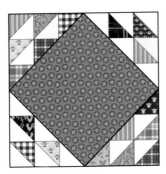

Make 4.

7. Arrange the blocks exactly as shown in the assembly diagram and sew them together in rows. Press the seam allowances in opposite directions from row to row. Sew the rows together. The Ocean Waves center should measure 24½" x 24½".

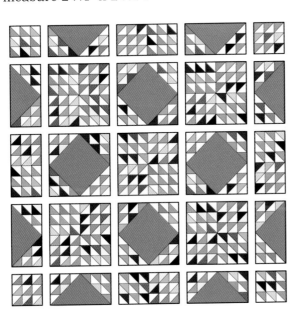

Making the Daisy Border

I used two machine-appliqué techniques on this quilt: interfacing appliqué and freezer paper with starch. The appliqués can be done using any method. You can do needle-turn appliqué or stitch the shapes by hand or machine after preparing them with freezer paper and starch. Follow the instructions here, referring to "Appliqué Techniques" (page 7), or use the method of your choice.

1. Make a circle template for the scallops using the pattern (page 90). Referring to "Interfacing Appliqué" (page 7), make 24 circles for the scallops by tracing the circle template onto the interfacing. Layer the interfacing with yellow print 2 and sew on the traced line. Trim to a scant ¼".

2. Fold a circle in half and finger press to make a crease for the centerline. Cut the circle in half on the crease, turn right side out, and press. Repeat for all the circles to make 48 scallops.

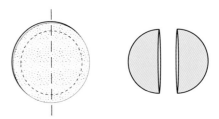

3. Place 12 scallops on each side of the pieced center, with right sides together and raw edges even. Pin and then baste the scallops in place.

4. Sew the 11" x 24½" pink print rectangles to the sides, sandwiching the yellow scallops in between. Sew the two 11" x 45½" pink rectangles to the top and bottom of the quilt. Press the scallops out and appliqué the curves in place by machine.

5. Make templates for the daisy petal, center, leaf, and stem using the patterns (page 90). Use a heat-resistant template material, such as Templar plastic (available at quilt shops), or use several layers of freezer paper ironed together for the shapes.

6. Use the daisy center template to cut 20 circles from assorted fabrics, adding a ¼" seam allowance as you cut.

7. Place the template in the center of a daisy center and sew a running stitch by hand in the seam allowance around the template. Pull the threads up to gather the fabric around the circle template.

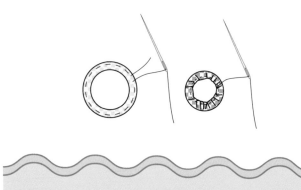

Handy Circle Template

Use a fiber faucet washer instead of a template when basting around the daisy centers. These are available in many sizes at hardware stores. For the daisy center, you need one with a 1¼" diameter.

8. Spray the circle with starch, press, and let cool. Remove the template. Stitch by hand or machine.

9. Prepare and appliqué the flower petals, leaves, and stems to the pink border using the method of your choice. Refer to the photograph (page 85) for placement guidance.

Making the Rickrack Border

1. Draw a diagonal line from corner to corner on the wrong side of the 2" yellow print 1 squares.

2. Sew two 2" yellow squares onto a 2" x 3¼" red print 2 rectangle as shown, stitching on the drawn line. Trim the corners off, leaving a ¼" seam allowance. Press toward the corner. Make 60 rickrack segments going in one direction and 60 in the opposite direction.

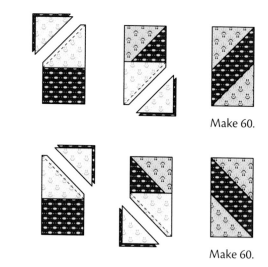

Make 60.

Make 60.

3. Sew the segments from step 2 into 60 pairs, and then sew 15 pairs together to make a border strip. Make four.

4. Fold the 1⅜" x 42" red print 2 strip and trim the selvage edge at a 45° angle. Cut four segments, 2" wide, at a 45° angle. (You will have eight total.) Refer to "Angled Cuts" (page 6) if needed to cut the 45° trapezoids.

1⅜"

2"

5. Assemble the four corners as shown, using the 2⅛" and 2⅜" yellow print 1 triangles and the 2" red print 2 angled segments. Press as shown. Join the units together to make four corner squares. Attach a corner square to each side of the top and bottom border strips.

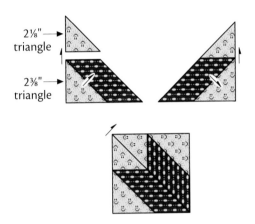

6. Sew the two border strips to the sides of the quilt, and then add the top and bottom borders.

Adding the Narrow Borders

1. You will have six strips for each narrow border; cut two of the strips of each color in half and add a half strip to each of the other four.

2. Sew five border strips together as shown to make one border unit. Make four units. Press the seam allowances in one direction.

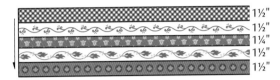

Make 4.

3. Refer to "Mitered Borders" (page 8) to add the border units to the quilt. The quilt should now measure 60½" x 60½".

Making the Outer Border

1. Draw a diagonal line from corner to corner on the wrong side of the 2½" light print squares.

2. Sew two 2½" light print squares onto a 2½" x 6½" red print 1 rectangle as shown, stitching on the drawn line. Trim the corners off, leaving a ¼" seam allowance. Press toward the corner. Make 60 units with red print 1; repeat to make 60 more using the pink print rectangles, sewing the squares in the opposite direction.

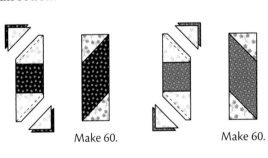

Make 60.   Make 60.

3. Sew 15 red units together with 15 pink units to make four border strips as shown.

Make 4.

4. For the corner blocks, layer the 2½" x 42" pink print and red print 1 strips with the pink strip on the bottom, wrong side up, and the red strip on top, right side up. Trim one end at a 45° angle. Cut into four 3⅜" segments at a 45° angle; you will have four of each color.

5. Sew a light print 2⅞" triangle to each 3⅜" segment as shown. Press. Add the 4⅞" light print triangles and press. Sew together to make the corner block; make four.

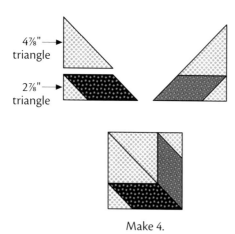

Make 4.

6. Sew a corner block from step 5 to each side of the top and bottom border strips.

7. Sew two border strips to the sides of the quilt; then add the top and bottom borders.

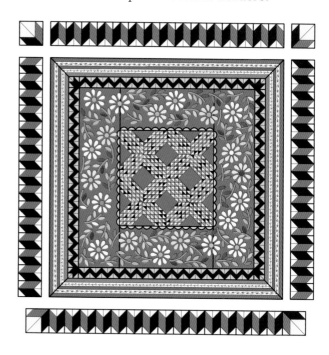

Finishing the Quilt

1. Press the quilt top carefully and mark it for quilting.

2. Layer the quilt top with the backing and batting. Baste with thread for hand quilting or with safety pins for machine quilting.

3. Quilt as desired and bind with the 2¼"-wide binding strips.

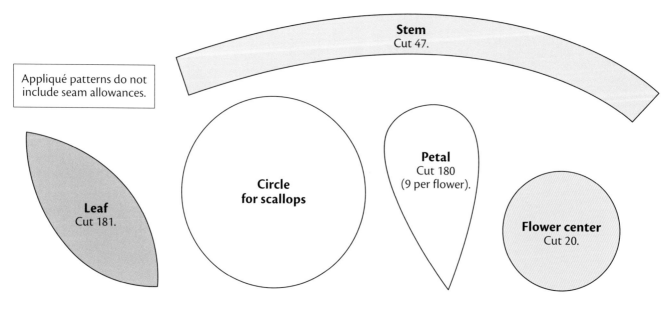

Appliqué patterns do not include seam allowances.

Stem
Cut 47.

Leaf
Cut 181.

Circle
for scallops

Petal
Cut 180
(9 per flower).

Flower center
Cut 20.

Dancing Ladies

Materials

Yardages are based on 42"-wide fabrics.

4¾ yards of light print for border

¼ yard *each* of 10 assorted prints for Nine Patch blocks*

1⅞ yards *total* of assorted light prints for alternate blocks and setting triangles

⅜ yard of black solid for appliqué (hair, arms, and shoes)

¼ yard of beige fabric for appliqué (head and hands)

28 pieces, 7" x 8", of assorted prints for skirts

28 pieces, 4½" x 5½", of assorted prints for aprons

Scraps of assorted prints for bodice, hats, and scarves

5¾ yards of fabric for backing

⅔ yard of fabric for binding

77" x 94" piece of batting

4 yards of fusible web

Appliqué pressing sheet (optional)

To simplify the cutting and piecing instructions, the materials list calls for 10 fabrics. If you want a scrappier quilt like the one shown, see "Using Scraps" at right.

Cutting

All measurements include a ¼"-wide seam allowance.

From *each* of the 10 assorted prints, cut:

3 strips, 2½" x 42" (30 total)

From the assorted light prints, cut:

35 squares, 6½" x 6½"

6 squares, 9¾" x 9¾"; cut each square twice diagonally to yield 24 side setting triangles

2 squares, 5½" x 5½"; cut each square once diagonally to yield 4 corner triangles

From the light print for border, cut on the *lengthwise* grain:

2 strips, 11½" x 72"

2 strips, 11½" x 76"

From the binding fabric, cut:

9 strips, 2¼" x 42"

Using Scraps

For a scrappier look, cut your full-width strips in half (2½" x 21") and pair them up with different fabrics to get more variety when using 10 fabrics. Or, choose smaller quantities of more fabrics. Three 2½" x 9" strips each of two different fabrics will make a 9"-long strip set. Cut three segments, 2½" wide, from each strip set to make two Nine Patch blocks.

On the bridge of Avignon
There they're dancing! There they're dancing!
On the bridge of Avignon
There they're dancing round and round.
–From *Nursery Friends from France*, translated by Olive Beaupré Miller

The quilt shown was made with French fabrics. For a different look, Civil
War–era reproduction prints will make the dancing girls look Early American.

Making the Nine Patch Blocks

1. Sew three 2½" x 42" strips *each* of two different assorted prints into strip sets as shown. Cut the strip sets into 15 segments, 2½" wide.

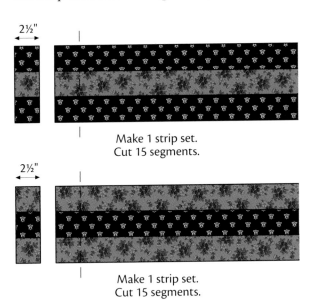

2½"

Make 1 strip set.
Cut 15 segments.

2½"

Make 1 strip set.
Cut 15 segments.

2. Sew two segments from one strip set and one segment from the other set to make a block. You can make up to 10 blocks from each pair of strip sets.

Make 5 of each.

3. Repeat steps 1 and 2 to make a total of 48 Nine Patch blocks.

Assembling the Quilt Center

1. Arrange the Nine Patch blocks and 6½" light print squares in diagonal rows as shown, adding side and corner setting triangles.

2. Sew the blocks and side setting triangles into rows and press toward the alternate blocks.

3. Sew the rows together. Press the seam allowances in one direction.

4. Add the corner triangles last. They are cut slightly oversized so that you can trim the corners to square them up.

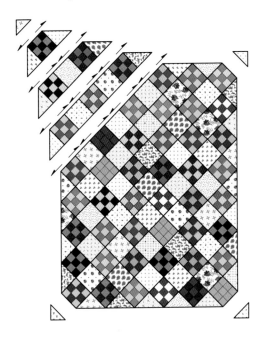

Appliquéing the Ladies to Borders

Refer to "Fusible Appliqué" (page 7) and follow the manufacturer's instructions for the fusible web that you are using.

Stay Organized

Because there are so many little pieces, I grouped all the hair, left arms, right arms, hands, and feet together and kept them in separate plastic storage bags marked left and right. When I was arranging the pieces, it was easy to find what I needed.

1. Using the patterns (page 95), prepare the skirts and aprons, and coordinate and prepare the three bodice pieces and the hats. I suggest using a nonstick appliqué pressing sheet to construct each of the ladies before placing them on the border. Trace the patterns to make a placement guide to help with arranging the appliqués.

2. Place and press seven ladies on the 11½" x 72" side borders. Begin by fusing one lady in the center. Fold the border strip in half and lightly crease to find and mark the center. Space the dancing ladies with hands approximately ½" apart.

Side border.
Make 2.

3. Repeat step 2 to fuse five ladies to the 11½" x 76" top and bottom borders. Note that four ladies will be appliquéd later after the borders are added to the quilt.

Top/bottom border.
Make 2.

4. Stitch around each piece before attaching the borders to the quilt. Stitch all like pieces at the same time so that you don't have to change thread color so often. For example, stitch all the black hair, arms, and shoes before changing to a different color thread.

Adding the Borders

1. Measure the length of the quilt through the center and trim the side borders to that measurement. Add to the quilt and press toward the borders.

2. Measure the width of the quilt through the center and trim the top and bottom borders to that measurement. Add to the quilt and press toward the borders.

3. Place, fuse, and stitch the four remaining dancing ladies to the corners.

Finishing the Quilt

1. Press the quilt top carefully and mark it for quilting.

2. Layer the quilt top with the backing and batting. Baste with thread for hand quilting or with safety pins for machine quilting.

3. Quilt as desired and bind with the 2¼"-wide binding strips.

A Quilting Tip

Consider stippling the quilt all over, but leave the ladies free of quilting.

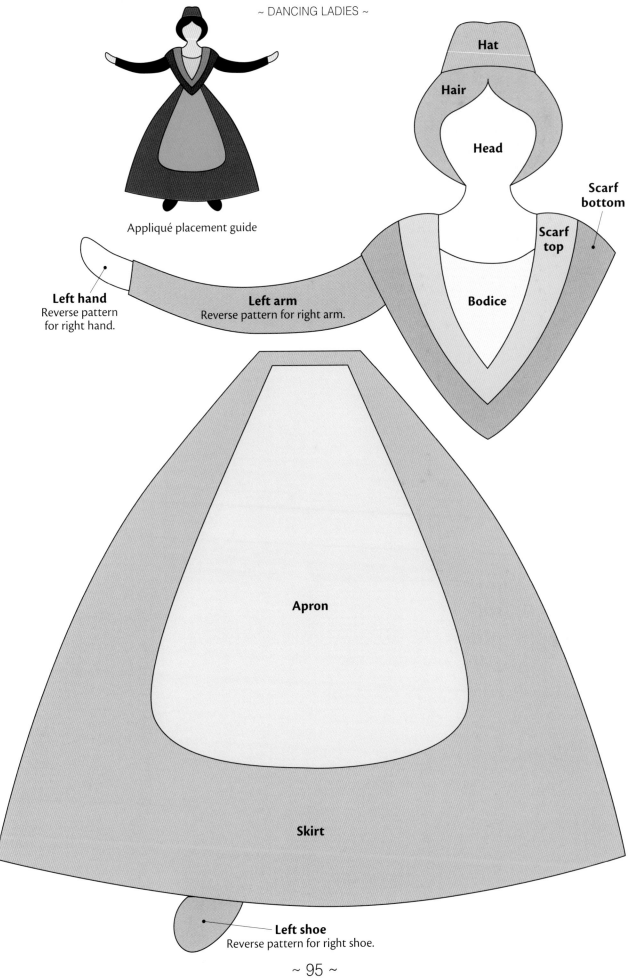

~ DANCING LADIES ~

Appliqué placement guide

Hat

Hair

Head

Scarf bottom

Scarf top

Bodice

Left hand
Reverse pattern
for right hand.

Left arm
Reverse pattern for right arm.

Apron

Skirt

Left shoe
Reverse pattern for right shoe.

About the Author

Born during World War II, Sandy grew up sewing in Holland, Michigan. "My mother taught me to sew on my grandmother's machine, and every time I finished a project she would say, 'Now, go show your father.' I always felt full approval from him and loved to see his reaction."

Sandy was trained as an art teacher and began quilting in 1979 while she was living in Iran and then Saudi Arabia, teaching at an American school. One of her first quilts was a baby quilt made for her third child, who was born in Saudi Arabia.

Back to California in 1984, Sandy continued to expand her interest in quilting and improve her skills. She started working at a local quilt store and began teaching classes. In 2000, she published a series of three quilt books with Jan Patek. In 2002, she started creating her own patterns and marketing them under the name American Jane Patterns. The following year she was invited to become a fabric designer for Moda Fabrics.

She has had quilts displayed at Houston Quilt Market and at the Pacific International Quilt Festival. She has created many fabric lines for Moda, and has 130 quilt patterns on display on her website, www.americanjane.com.